LISA THOMAS   MARTHA SWIFT

PRIMROSE BAKERY

CELEBRATIONS

SQUARE PEG

PRIMROSE BAKERY
CELEBRATIONS

FOR KEVIN AND DANIEL

CONTENTS

INTRODUCTION   6

Young Girl's Party   *12*

YOUNG BOY'S PARTY   34

TEENAGE PARTY   **52**

PICNICS   **70**

Baby Shower   *90*

Afternoon Tea Party   112

COCKTAILS & CUPCAKES   134

Christmas and New Year   *168*

ACKNOWLEDGEMENTS   202

INDEX   204

INTRODUCTION

The Primrose Bakery Book was published in October 2011, eight years after we started Primrose Bakery. It was a comprehensive guide to everything we do at the bakeries on a daily basis and also gave people a snapshot of daily life at either one of our shops. Our staff, children, customers, fellow business owners and animals are all as important to our business as we are, and without them all we would not have come as far as we have.

With this, our third book, we wanted to do something slightly different. We decided this time to move away from the things we produce on a daily basis and open the book up to a series of occasions where the cake or cakes remain the centrepiece, but the accompanying food and the setting also become important. With a combination of new recipes and ideas for how to put all the elements together and display them, we hope to provide our readers with inspiration for celebrations of their own.

We are lucky to employ some very talented chefs and other staff who help us to develop and test all our new recipes. All the staff (and some of the customers) give their feedback and opinions before we finalize them. It can be quite a slow process, but we would never want to put our names to recipes we would not happily use ourselves in our shops or at home. We always keep them as easy and simple as possible, using seasonal and natural ingredients wherever we can, and also ingredients that can be found easily online or in the local supermarket.

For locations we have used our two shops, but have also gone out and about to some of the places in London that we love and use on a regular basis and feel are closely affiliated to what we do. Again, they are there both to serve as ideas for your own celebrations and to show some of the amazing places on our doorstep.

Running a small business remains a challenge even after so many years. It is certainly a full-time commitment that is both hugely rewarding and enjoyable but also sometimes exhausting and worrying. The best parts of our job remain our customers and the positive feedback they give us, and the fact that in eight years we have been able to open two shops and write three books and an App.

We are hoping to open our third shop in 2013 and possibly one more after that, although we never want Primrose Bakery to be a 'chain', as we worry that it might lose the principles we first started with. Opening a new shop is a huge undertaking, both financially and emotionally, but we feel we have a dedicated and hard-working team of staff who can help us do it. Our children are all growing up very fast, which makes it much easier than when we first started – and they are now all used to us not being around very much and, on many occasions, to the cakes coming first.

Starting a cake business is considered by many to be a dream job, and of course in very many ways it is. The business we run now is so different in size to the one the two of us started eight years ago. With no formal training in either running a business or catering it was perhaps a foolish venture, although even with the benefit of hindsight we would probably have done it anyway.

We hope that this book gives you plenty of ideas and inspiration for more home baking and for the occasions we have chosen to feature. We have really enjoyed developing new and quite unusual recipes for this book and it has reminded us how rewarding baking and running our business continues to be.

www.primrosebakery.co.uk

For sweet treats on the go download The Primrose Bakery App from iTunes

Young Girl's Party

We have taken our inspiration for our young girl's party from the many cakes and cupcakes we make for our youngest customers, for Martha's daughters Daisy and Millie on their birthdays, and from things we both enjoyed in our own childhood. We have chosen quite a pink, pretty theme and used our shop in Primrose Hill as the backdrop.

Puffed Rice Doughnut Cake

A very simple but amazingly delicious birthday cake that anyone of any age would find hard to resist. You will need a Big Top Donut silicone baking tin or similar mould for this cake.

Discard the central piece of silicone and spray the inside of each of the moulds lightly with the oil spray.

First, melt together the butter and marshmallows. To use the hob, melt the butter in a large pan over a low heat. Add the marshmallows and stir until they have also fully melted. To use a microwave, melt the butter in a heatproof bowl for 5–10 seconds. Stir then repeat until melted. Add the marshmallows to the bowl and microwave again for about 1½–2 minutes, until the marshmallows are soft and liquid.

Add the puffed rice to the marshmallow mixture and fold through with a wooden spoon until everything is combined. Divide this mixture evenly between the two moulds. Gently press the mixture into the moulds until the surfaces are even, using a piece of greaseproof paper to avoid getting your hands stuck to it.

Place one half of the mould on top of the other and press down gently. Leave to set in the mould for at least one hour or until the mixture hardens. You can speed up the process by putting it into the refrigerator.

Remove the cake from the mould (it should come out easily), and prepare the icing. Beat all the ingredients together with an electric hand beater until smooth. Spoon over the doughnut, allowing the icing to drip down the sides. Sprinkle with hundreds and thousands or decorate with sweets.

Makes one 20cm doughnut-shaped cake, serving approximately 12–15

FOR THE CAKE
oil spray
80g unsalted butter
300g marshmallows
225g puffed rice

FOR THE ICING
350g icing sugar
1–2 tablespoons boiling water
1 tablespoon cocoa powder, or to taste
hundreds and thousands or sweets, to decorate

Bubblegum Cupcakes

Makes 12 regular cupcakes

**110g unsalted butter, at
   room temperature**
**225g caster sugar, preferably
   golden**
**2 large eggs, free-range or
   organic**
**1 teaspoon good-quality
   vanilla extract**
120ml semi-skimmed milk
125g plain flour
150g self-raising flour
12 teaspoons pink sprinkles

Preheat the oven to 180°C/160°C (fan)/350°F/gas 4. Line a 12-hole muffin tray with muffin cases.

Cream the butter and sugar in a bowl until the mixture is pale and smooth. Add the eggs, one at a time, mixing briefly after each addition. This can take a few minutes. Scrape down the sides of the bowl with a rubber spatula from time to time to ensure the mixture stays well combined.

Add the vanilla extract to the milk in a plastic measuring jug. In a separate bowl, combine the two flours.

Add one-third of the flours to the combined butter and sugar mixture and beat well. Pour in one-third of the milk and beat again. Repeat these steps until all the flour and milk has been added.

Carefully spoon the mixture evenly into the muffin cases. To each one add 1 teaspoon of pink sprinkles and swirl into the batter very gently.

Bake in the centre of the oven for approximately 25 minutes, until slightly raised and golden brown. You will be able to see the pink sprinkles through the cooked cupcake. Remove from the oven and leave in the tray for 10 minutes or so, then place carefully on a wire rack to cool. While they are cooling make the buttercream icing (see page 18). When completely cool, they are ready to ice.

The cupcakes can be stored in airtight containers for up to 3 days at room temperature. Do not refrigerate.

Bubblegum Buttercream Icing

Makes enough to ice 15–20 regular cupcakes

115g unsalted butter, at room temperature
60ml semi-skimmed milk
½ teaspoon bubblegum oil extract, or to taste
   (we use LorAnn Oils bubble gum flavour)
500g icing sugar, sifted
a few drops of pink food colouring
pink sprinkles (optional)
gumballs or pieces of wrapped bubblegum to decorate

In a mixing bowl, beat the butter, milk, bubblegum oil and half the icing sugar together until smooth. This will usually take a few minutes. Gradually add the remainder of the icing sugar to produce a buttercream of a creamy and smooth consistency.

Add a few drops of pink colouring and beat well. We tend to stick to a pale pink shade but you can make it as pink as you like!

The buttercream can be stored in an airtight container for up to 3 days at room temperature. Beat well before re-using.

Ice each cupcake with some of the buttercream and decorate with pink sprinkles, if using, and a piece of bubblegum in the centre.

White Chocolate Cupcakes

Makes 12 regular cupcakes

115g white chocolate
100g unsalted butter, at
** room temperature**
100g granulated sugar
2 large eggs, free-range
** or organic, separated**
1 teaspoon good-quality
** vanilla extract**
155g plain flour
1 teaspoon bicarbonate
** of soda**
115g buttermilk

*White chocolate is one of those things you either love or hate,
so these cupcakes will have a mixed reception. Whatever
your preference, they look divine!*

Preheat the oven to 180°C/160°C (fan)/350°F/gas 4. Line a 12-hole muffin tray with muffin cases.

Break the white chocolate into small pieces and melt, either in the microwave on a medium heat at 10–20 second intervals, stirring well in between, or in a heatproof bowl over a pan of simmering water on the hob, making sure the bowl doesn't touch the water. Be careful not to burn the chocolate. It should be smooth and creamy when melted. Set aside to cool slightly.

Cream the butter and sugar in a bowl until the mixture is light and fluffy. Beat in the egg yolks one at a time, then stir in the melted chocolate and vanilla extract. Gradually beat in the flour and bicarbonate of soda alternately with the buttermilk, mixing until just incorporated.

In a separate bowl, beat the egg whites until stiff peaks form. Fold one-third of them into the batter with a metal spoon and then quickly fold in the remainder until no white streaks can be seen.

Carefully spoon the mixture evenly into the muffin cases. Bake in the centre of the oven for approximately 25 minutes, until slightly raised and golden brown. Check with a cake skewer in the centre of one of the cakes to see that they are cooked – the skewer should come out clean. Remove from the oven and leave in the tray for 10 minutes or so, then place carefully on a wire rack to cool before icing.

The cupcakes can be stored in airtight containers for up to 3 days at room temperature. Do not refrigerate.

White Chocolate Icing

Makes enough for 12 regular cupcakes

100g white chocolate
55g unsalted butter, at room temperature
30ml semi-skimmed milk, at room temperature
½ teaspoon good-quality vanilla extract
250g icing sugar, sifted
3 tablespoons double cream
grated or shaved white chocolate, to decorate

Melt the chocolate as for the white chocolate cupcake recipe (see page 23). Leave to cool slightly.

Combine all the ingredients, apart from the melted chocolate, cream and decoration, in a large bowl and beat well until smooth and creamy. Add the chocolate and double cream and beat well again.

It is best to use this icing on the cupcakes straight away. If it stiffens too much, soften with a bit more double cream or put it into the microwave for 10 seconds, then beat well again before using.

This icing needs to be stored in the fridge because it contains cream, but it will become solid. To bring it back to the right consistency, microwave it to a fairly liquid form, beat well and then let it sit out for a while before using. If you don't microwave it enough it has a tendency to become lumpy when you re-beat.

Ice each cupcake with some of the icing and decorate with some grated white chocolate or shaved white chocolate curls.

Confetti Cake

Makes one 3-layer 20cm cake

315g self-raising flour
35g cornflour
1½ teaspoons baking powder
335g golden caster sugar
6 large eggs, preferably
free-range or organic
335g unsalted butter, at
room temperature
5 tablespoons milk
1½ teaspoons good-quality
vanilla extract
¾ teaspoon red food colouring
1½ tablespoons multi-
coloured sprinkles or
hundreds and thousands

By using multicoloured sprinkles through the batter and colouring the layers different shades, you will create a pretty and fun cake that would delight any child for a party or teatime.

Preheat the oven to 180°C/160°C (fan)/350°F/gas 4. Grease and line three 20cm sandwich baking tins.

Put the flour, cornflour, baking powder and sugar into a food processor and pulse to combine. Add the eggs, butter, milk and vanilla extract and pulse briefly until combined, but do not overmix. Divide the batter evenly between three bowls. It may be best to use bowls that are the same size and to weigh them with the batter in, so that you can be sure you will end up with three sponge layers of the same size.

Add ¼ teaspoon of red food colouring to one of the bowls and ½ teaspoon to the second one. Leave the third one uncoloured. Briefly beat the mixture in the first two bowls to allow the colour to disperse through the batter. Add ½ tablespoon of sprinkles to each bowl and stir to mix them through evenly, then pour each bowl of batter into each of the prepared tins.

Bake in the oven for about 20–25 minutes. If possible, put all three tins on the middle shelf. If not, you may find it a good idea to rotate the tins between the shelves while cooking. Check that the cakes are cooked by inserting a skewer into the centre of each one, it should come out clean. Remove the cakes from the oven and leave them to cool in their tins for about 10 minutes before turning out to cool fully on a wire rack. Once the cakes are completely cool, decorate with the pink vanilla buttercream icing (see page 26).

Pink Vanilla Buttercream Icing

230g unsalted butter, at room temperature
120ml semi-skimmed milk
2 teaspoons good-quality vanilla extract
1kg icing sugar, sifted
a few drops of pink food colouring
multicoloured sprinkles or
    hundreds and thousands (optional)

Beat the butter, milk, vanilla extract and half the icing sugar until smooth. This usually takes a few minutes. Gradually add the remainder of the icing sugar to produce a buttercream with a creamy and smooth consistency. Mix in a couple of drops of pink colouring and beat again, adding a few more drops if necessary until you reach your preferred shade.

When you are ready to assemble the cake, peel the greaseproof paper from the base of each sponge and put one layer on your serving plate. Spread with a thin layer of the buttercream icing, then put another sponge layer on top and repeat. Finally, place the third layer of cake on top and cover the top and sides with the rest of the icing. Either leave undecorated or scatter sprinkles over the top.

Sprinkle-covered Ice-cream Sandwiches

Makes approximately 20 circles, or 10 finished sandwiches

225g unsalted butter, at room temperature
225g golden caster sugar
4 heaped tablespoons golden syrup
340g self-raising flour
115g cornflour
115g cocoa
a tub of good-quality vanilla ice-cream
multicoloured sprinkles or hundreds and thousands

Using our favourite bourbon biscuits from our bakery, this is a very easy and colourful recipe to liven up a child's birthday party or any teatime.

Preheat the oven to 180°C/160°C (fan)/350°F/gas 4.

Cream the butter, sugar and syrup together in a mixer. In a separate bowl sift the flour, cornflour and cocoa together, then beat into the creamed mixture together with 4 tablespoons of water. If the mixture seems very dry add a little more water. Knead thoroughly to form a smooth, thick dough.

You can either rest the dough in the fridge until you are ready to finish making the biscuits, or roll it out straight away. Once you are ready to go, line a flat baking tray with greaseproof paper, then lightly flour a work surface and roll out the dough to a thickness of 3 or 4mm. Using the base of a largish tumbler-type glass cutter, cut into circles. Transfer each circle onto the tray, leaving a little space between each one.

Bake in the oven for approximately 12–14 minutes, until firm to the touch. Make sure you don't overcook them, as they will burn. Remove from the oven and transfer to a wire rack and allow to cool completely before filling.

Ten minutes before you're ready to assemble the biscuits, take the ice cream out of the freezer to soften a little and pour the sprinkles into a large bowl or plate.

Sandwich two biscuits together with quite a thick layer of vanilla ice-cream and lay on a plate. When they are all filled, roll each sandwich on its side through the sprinkles, thereby fully coating the ice-cream middle of the biscuits.

Ideally these sandwiches should be eaten almost immediately or on the day they are made, when they are at their freshest and before the ice-cream melts. If you do store them, make sure they are kept in an airtight container in the freezer.

Ice-cream Floats

Makes one ice-cream float

**2 or 3 scoops of good-quality
vanilla ice-cream**
**1 can or small bottle of
cola or cream soda**

Using an ice-cream scoop, put
the ice-cream into a tall glass
and then carefully pour the
cola or cream soda over
the top to fill the glass. It will
fizz up considerably, so pour
slowly! Serve with a tall spoon
and a straw.

Fairy Bread

Fairy bread was, and still is, a staple of New Zealand and Australian children's birthday parties. Lisa's birthdays growing up were notable for the cakes her mother created and the different shapes she cut the fairy bread into.

Fairy bread is, of course, the simplest of things, but holds a little magic as it is only to be eaten on birthdays. Tempted as Lisa has been on those occasions when the grocery shopping hasn't been done, the fridge is bare and peanut butter is off the menu because of allergies, she still hasn't succumbed to adding it to her sons' lunchboxes as this would be against the law!

So to make only on those very special days, you need:

1 loaf of sliced white bread
butter
hundreds and thousands

Butter each slice of bread, then cut off the crusts or use a cookie cutter to make shapes in each slice. Carefully tip the hundreds and thousands onto a plate or bowl and dip each piece of bread, buttered side down, into them to coat them fully.

BUTTER £1·70
WITH HONEY £1·70
SPRINKLES
RUIT SALAD £3·4
TH YOGHURT £3·4
WITH FRUIT AND YOGHURT £3·4
£3·50
OF ORGANIC
MILK
£1·25

YOUNG BOY'S PARTY

An American diner-type theme is perfect for boys, although many girls would be equally happy with this theme. Cupcakes are thought of as very American in flavour and style, and many of the recipes we have included here really show off the American side to what we do.

PUFFED RICE GUMBALL CAKE

We decided to include this gumball machine-shaped cake to show just how easy it is to be creative and speedy without having to spend too much money. You can, of course, use any cake tin or mould to create any shape you desire. Start with the same quantities as for the Puffed Rice Doughnut Cake (see page 14) and adjust as needed depending on the size of the tin. We used a Wilton Gumball Machine tin.

160g unsalted butter
600g marshmallows (the big American white marshmallows
work well, although pink ones would be fine too)
450g puffed rice
oil spray
gumball sweets

Prepare the puffed rice mixture using the method shown for the Puffed Rice Doughnut Cake (see page 14).

To create the shape, put the gumball sweets into the tin and then pack the puffed rice mixture around them.

To make the shapes 3D remove the first half from the tin once it has set hard and repeat the whole process. While the second half is still a little tacky, stick the two halves together.

There are so many possible alternatives with this recipe. Try adding different flavours, such as chocolate or peanut butter chips, and as for decorating, piping bags or icing pens, sweets and melted chocolate are all you need.

PEANUT BUTTER AND JELLY CUPCAKES

Lisa's son Ned is a big fan of Goober's peanut butter and jelly, so we were inspired to create a cupcake version. It works very well for an American-themed party.

Makes 12 regular cupcakes

120g plain flour
1 teaspoon baking powder
a pinch of salt
75g unsalted butter, at room temperature
130g crunchy peanut butter
190g soft light brown sugar
2 large eggs
1 teaspoon vanilla extract
60ml milk
60g grape jelly (we use Goober)
milk chocolate icing (see page 39)
jelly beans, to decorate

Preheat the oven to 180°C/160°C (fan)/350°F/gas 4. Line a 12-hole muffin tray with muffin cases. Combine the flour, baking powder and salt in a bowl.

In a separate bowl, cream the butter, peanut butter and sugar with an electric hand beater until well blended. Add the eggs and vanilla extract and beat well, then add some of the flour mixture and a little milk alternately until they are well incorporated and the batter is smooth.

Divide the mixture evenly between the muffin cases and bake in the centre of the oven for approximately 20 minutes, until raised and golden brown in colour. Remove from the oven and leave in the tray for 10 minutes, then place on a wire rack to cool.

When completely cool, scoop out a teaspoon of sponge from the centre of each cupcake and fill with grape jelly. Ice with the milk chocolate icing to finish.

MILK CHOCOLATE ICING

Makes enough for 12 regular cupcakes

**300g good-quality milk
  chocolate, broken into
  small pieces**
60ml double cream
**2 tablespoons unsalted butter,
  at room temperature**
½ teaspoon vanilla extract

Melt the chocolate, either in the microwave on a medium heat at 10–20 second intervals and stirring well in between, or in a heatproof bowl over a pan of simmering water on the hob, making sure the bowl doesn't touch the water. Be careful not to burn the chocolate.

Add the cream, butter and vanilla to the melted chocolate and stir well to combine. Allow to cool. Put the bowl in the fridge for about 30 minutes to set a little, then beat well before using to ice the cupcakes.

COLA CUPCAKES

These cupcakes proved hard to perfect and we had several tastings before we got them right. We found that using a cola concentrate rather than real cola is much more effective.

Makes 12 regular cupcakes

125g unsalted butter, at room temperature
115g golden caster sugar
2 large free-range or organic eggs
235g self-raising flour
¼ teaspoon salt
65ml cola concentrate (we use SodaStream)
65ml milk

Preheat the oven to 180°C/160°C (fan)/ 350°F/gas 4. Line a 12-hole muffin tray with muffin cases.

Cream the butter and sugar in a bowl until the mixture is pale and fluffy. Add the eggs, one at a time, mixing briefly after each addition. Sift the flour and salt on top of the mix and beat until just combined.

Pour in the cola concentrate and milk and beat until well incorporated. Scrape down the sides of the bowl with a rubber spatula to ensure the mixture stays well combined.

Divide the mixture evenly into the cases and bake in the centre of the oven for approximately 20 minutes, until raised and golden brown in colour. Remove from the oven and leave in the tray for 10 minutes, then place on a wire rack to cool.

COLA ICING

Makes enough for 12 regular cupcakes

125g unsalted butter, at room temperature
300g icing sugar
60g cola concentrate
juice of ½ a lime
sugar cola bottles to decorate

Combine all the ingredients in a bowl and beat until smooth. If the icing is a bit stiff add a little more lime juice to achieve the desired spreading consistency.

Ice each cupcake with some of the buttercream and top with a sugar cola bottle.

TRES LECHES CAKE

Makes one 3-layer, 20cm cake

FOR THE CAKE
390g plain flour
2 teaspoons baking powder
1 teaspoon salt
225g unsalted butter,
    at room temperature
410g granulated sugar
10 large free-range eggs
3 teaspoons vanilla extract

FOR THE GLAZE
1 x 410g tin of evaporated
    milk
1 x 400g tin of condensed
    milk
125g white rum
125g double cream

FOR THE ICING
125g desiccated coconut
4 tablespoons icing sugar,
    plus 1 teaspoon
600ml whipping or double
    cream

This traditional Mexican cake, whose name means 'three milks', was first discovered by Lisa in the summer of 2011 when she was on holiday in Tulum, Mexico. We have all become addicted to the cool, milk-drenched sponge and sweet cream, which brings a delicious relief from the midday sun or after a fiery chilli feast. It also proved very popular in our shops as soon as it first appeared on the counters.

Make the cakes the day before you eat them, as they need to sit overnight in the fridge.

Preheat the oven to 190°C/170°fan/ 375°F/gas 5. Grease and line three 20cm sandwich cake tins.

In a bowl, combine the flour, baking powder and salt.

In a separate bowl, beat the butter and sugar together very briefly until just combined. Add the eggs, one at a time, and beat to combine. Beat in the vanilla extract, then add the dry ingredients in three stages, mixing to combine only. It is essential not to overmix.

Divide the mixture evenly between the three tins. Each tin should have approximately 550g of batter in it. Bake the layers in the oven for 20–25 minutes, until golden brown and an inserted skewer comes out clean. Remove from the oven and allow to cool in their tins for half an hour while you make the glaze.

To make the glaze, simply mix all the ingredients together in a bowl. Leaving the cakes in their tins, prick them all over with a fork and pour an equal amount of the glaze over each one, covering the surface of each cake. Leave the cakes in their tins in the fridge overnight to let the liquid soak in.

When you are ready to assemble the cake the next day, preheat the oven to 180°C/160°C (fan)/ 350°F/gas 4. Spread the coconut and one teaspoon of icing sugar on a piece of parchment paper on a baking tray and toast in the oven for about 7 minutes, until golden brown. Allow to cool.

Whip together the cream and the 4 tablespoons of icing sugar. Place one of the cake layers on a plate and cover the surface with approximately one-quarter of the cream mixture. Place the next layer on top and repeat with a layer of the cream mixture. Place the third cake on top and then spread the remaining cream mixture all over the top and sides of the cake. Sprinkle the cooled toasted coconut over the sides and top of the cake to decorate.

If there is any cake left over, it must be stored in the fridge as it contains fresh cream. As the sponge is so moist, there will not be any problems with it drying out as with other sponges.

MEXICAN CHOCOLATE SPICED CUPCAKES

Authentic Mexican chocolate is made from selected cacao beans and traditionally infused with cinnamon. This has a richer and spicier flavour than regular plain chocolate. We add even more cinnamon to this recipe for an even bigger flavour! We love Casa Mexico in Bethnal Green, which stocks a great range of authentic Mexican products, but you can add your own spices to any good chocolate.

Makes 18 regular cupcakes

250g unsalted butter
210g Mexican chocolate (we use Ibarra)
330ml milk
185g golden caster sugar
105g plain flour
105g self-raising flour
40g cocoa
2 teaspoons ground cinnamon
3 eggs, lightly beaten

Preheat the oven to 180°C/160° (fan)/375°F/gas 5. Line 2 muffin trays with muffin cases.

Melt the butter and chocolate, either in the microwave on a medium heat at 10–20 second intervals and stirring well in between, or in a heatproof bowl over a pan of simmering water on the hob, making sure the bowl doesn't touch the water. Be careful not to burn the chocolate. The mixture will still have grains of sugar in it.

Remove from the heat and stir in the milk until well combined, then add the sugar. Sift the flours, cocoa and cinnamon directly in to the batter and fold until well mixed. Add the eggs and beat until combined.

Spoon the mixture into the cases, filling each case about two-thirds full. Bake in the oven for 20–25 minutes, or until a skewer comes out clean when inserted.

Remove from the oven and leave in the tray for 5 minutes and then take out to cool. Do not leave the cupcakes in the tray to cool completely as the condensation will cause the paper to pull away from the cakes.

SPICED CHOCOLATE BUTTERCREAM ICING

350g good-quality dark chocolate (at least 70% cocoa solids)
1 teaspoon ground cinnamon
225g unsalted butter, at room temperature
250g icing sugar, sifted
1 tablespoon semi-skimmed milk
1 teaspoon good-quality vanilla extract

Melt the chocolate, either in the microwave on a medium heat at 10-20 second intervals and stirring well in between, or in a heatproof bowl over a pan of simmering water on the hob, making sure the bowl doesn't touch the water, until smooth and a thick pouring consistency. Be careful not to burn the chocolate. Leave to cool slightly then beat in the cinnamon.

In a separate bowl beat the butter, sugar, milk and vanilla extract with an electric hand beater until smooth. Add the melted chocolate and beat until thick and creamy.

This icing can be stored in an airtight container at room temperature for up to three days. Remember to beat well before re-using. If it looks too runny, simply keep beating – this will thicken the icing and improve its consistency.

CHOCOLATE CHILLI AND COFFEE ICE-CREAM SANDWICHES

Makes two 33 x 23cm thin single layers to sandwich together

100g plain flour
100g self-raising flour
¼ teaspoon salt
½ teaspoon cayenne pepper
½ teaspoon ground cinnamon
100g unsalted butter
100g dark chocolate (at least 70% cocoa solids)
125g soft brown sugar
100g milk
2 eggs, lightly beaten
3 litres good-quality coffee-flavoured ice-cream

A perfect combination of hot chilli chocolate and cool coffee ice-cream, these sandwiches balance the other party food brilliantly.

Preheat the oven to 190°C/170°C (fan)/375°F/ gas 5. Grease the baking trays and line with parchment paper.

Sift the flours together in a bowl and add the salt, cayenne pepper and cinnamon.

Melt the butter and dark chocolate in a heatproof bowl placed over a pan of simmering water on the hob, making sure the bowl doesn't touch the water. Remove from the heat, add the sugar and stir until all combined.

Pour in the milk and mix until just combined. Add the dry ingredients and beat or whisk until these are also all combined. Add the eggs and beat again.

Split the batter equally between the two trays and spread evenly over the base of each one. They will be fairly shallow layers. Bake for 5–8 minutes, or until a skewer comes out clean. Remove from the oven and leave the cakes to cool slightly in the tray, then turn out on to wire racks to cool completely.

TO ASSEMBLE THE ICE-CREAM SANDWICHES

Take the ice-cream out of the freezer and place in the fridge 1 hour prior to assembly.

Reline your baking tray with clean parchment paper. Put one layer of the cake back into the lined tray and spread the softened ice-cream evenly over the top. Cover with clingfilm and put it into the freezer for 2 hours so that the ice-cream hardens a little.

After 2 hours, remove the tray from the freezer and place the second layer of cake on top of the ice cream. Press down gently to ensure the cake is in contact with the ice cream, then cover with clingfilm and return to the freezer for a minimum of 4 hours or overnight. When you are ready to serve, cut into pieces with a serrated knife.

CHOCOLATE CHILLI MOUSTACHE CAKE

We've used the same sponge as for the chocolate and coffee ice-cream sandwiches on page 61 for this recipe, but this time we have made it into a moustache shape and iced it all over with chocolate icing! Moustaches are enjoying a resurgence and are perfectly in keeping with our Mexican theme.

Makes one 13 x 9cm rectangular single layer cake

250g plain flour
250g self-raising flour
¾ teaspoon salt
1¼ teaspoons cayenne pepper
1¼ teaspoons ground cinnamon
250g unsalted butter
250g good-quality dark chocolate
   (at least 70% cocoa solids)
315g soft brown sugar
250g milk
5 eggs, lightly beaten

Preheat the oven to 190°C/170°C (fan)/375°F/gas 5. Grease and line the baking tray with parchment paper.

Sift the flours together in a bowl and add the salt, cayenne pepper and cinnamon.

Melt the butter and dark chocolate in a heatproof bowl placed over a pan of simmering water on the hob, making sure the bowl doesn't touch the water. Remove from the heat, add the sugar and stir until all combined.

Pour in the milk and mix until just combined. Add the dry ingredients and beat or whisk until these are also all combined. Add the eggs and beat again.

Pour the batter into the baking tin making sure it is spread evenly. Bake for 20–25 minutes, or until an inserted skewer comes out clean. Remove from the oven and leave to cool slightly in the tin before turning it out on to a wire rack to cool completely.

CHOCOLATE BUTTERCREAM ICING

Makes enough for 12 regular cupcakes

350g good-quality dark chocolate (at least 70% cocoa solids)
225g unsalted butter, at room temperature
250g icing sugar, sifted
1 tablespoon semi-skimmed milk
1 teaspoon good-quality vanilla extract

Melt the chocolate, either in the microwave on a medium heat at 10–20 second intervals and stirring well in between, or in a bowl over a pan of simmering water on the hob, making sure the bowl doesn't touch the water, until smooth and a thick pouring consistency. Be careful not to burn the chocolate. Remove from the heat and leave to cool slightly.

In a separate bowl, beat the butter, icing sugar, milk and vanilla with an electric hand beater until smooth. Add the melted chocolate and beat until thick and creamy.

Create the template of a moustache on some parchment paper – lay it on top of the cake and carefully cut round it with a very sharp knife. Discard or eat the cake that is cut away. Put the moustache-shaped sponge onto a cake board or flat plate and ice all over the top and sides to completely cover the cake.

CHEESE QUESADILLAS

Makes 4

4 flour tortillas
oil spray
200g grated medium
 Cheddar (or your favourite
 cheese)

A very simple Mexican variation on a toasted cheese sandwich, these have mass appeal and are delicious served alongside the guacamole and some Mexican sodas or cola.

Spray both sides of one tortilla with oil and place it in a frying pan over a low heat. Sprinkle approximately 50g of cheese over one half of the tortilla. Try not to get it too close to the edges. Fold the other half of the tortilla over the cheese.

Cook for approximately 1–2 minutes, or until golden brown. To check, use a spatula and gently lift the corner of the tortilla to see its underside. Once it is golden brown, flip the tortilla/quesadilla onto the other side and cook for a further minute and a half, or until golden brown. The cheese should be melted and gooey.

Once cooked, use a spatula to transfer the quesadilla to a plate and cut it in half to serve. Repeat the same process with the other tortillas.

GUACAMOLE

There's nothing that counters the sweetness of the cakes better than some very salty tortilla chips dipped in guacamole. This recipe comes from our chef Julia and tastes even better served with authentic Mexican corn chips.

Serves 5–6

1 small tomato
½ small red onion
1 garlic clove
2 ripe avocados
juice of 1 lime
a pinch of salt
a few chilli flakes (optional)
2–3 sprigs of fresh coriander
   (plus more for decoration if wanted)
tortilla corn chips, to serve

Cut the tomato in half, remove all the seeds and juice and chop into tiny pieces. Place in a mixing bowl. Dice the red onion into tiny pieces and add to the tomato. Crush the garlic and add to the bowl.

Remove the skin and stones of the avocados, mash the flesh with a fork and add to the ingredients in the bowl. Add the lime juice, salt and chilli flakes, if using, and mix together well with a fork until combined.

Finely chop the coriander and add to the bowl. Taste, and adjust any seasoning accordingly. Store in the fridge until needed.

Serve the guacamole with a big bowl of tortilla chips.

MEXICAN CORN ON THE COB (ELOTE)

Makes 12 corn cobs

12 corn cobs
30g unsalted butter
a pinch of cayenne pepper
2 tablespoons mayonnaise
40g finely grated mature
Cheddar
30g finely grated Parmesan
2 limes, cut into wedges,
to serve

This spicy, cheesy corn on the cob is inspired by the ones served at the amazing Café Habana in New York and is best eaten on the street with one of their fresh lemonades in the hot sunshine. It works well at a party to counter the sweetness of the cakes without being too filling.

Preheat the oven to 180°C/160°C (fan)/350°F/gas 4.

Wrap each corn cob in aluminium foil. Place on a baking tray and bake for 35–40 minutes. Alternatively, grill the corn on a barbecue for 7–10 minutes, turning regularly.

Melt the butter in a heatproof bowl in the microwave or in a small pan on the hob. Once melted, sprinkle with the cayenne pepper and stir in the mayonnaise.

In a separate bowl, combine the two cheeses.

Once the corn cobs are cooked, unwrap them and brush on the butter mixture. Sprinkle the cheese mix over the top and serve with lime wedges.

PICNICS

Picnics and the British weather do not always go hand in hand. Especially, it would seem, while we have been writing this book, which has come at a time of almost daily rain over the past few months. However, the British love picnics and on a rare sunny day there is nothing nicer than sitting outside with friends and family, everyone bringing along a different dish.

Food for picnics needs to be easily transportable and able to be eaten at room temperature. It should also be light and summery in its flavours and as simple as possible to prepare. The following recipes have been chosen with all this in mind, and hopefully we will all be enjoying eating them outside on many occasions!

COCONUT AND ELDERFLOWER CAKE

This is one of the most recent flavour combinations we've been experimenting with at Primrose Bakery. We have been selling it in cupcake form in our shops, but we think it also works really well as a large cake for a picnic – either way, it is delicious and very summery in flavour.

Makes one 20cm layer cake

225g unsalted butter, at room temperature
225g golden caster sugar
3 eggs, lightly beaten
150g plain flour
105g desiccated coconut
1 ½ teaspoons baking powder
½ teaspoon salt
105ml elderflower cordial
105ml milk

Preheat the oven to 180°C/160°C (fan)/350°F/gas mark 4. Grease and line the bases of two 20cm sandwich cake tins.

Cream the butter and sugar in a large bowl until light and fluffy. Add the eggs and beat for a further minute, using an electric hand beater on medium speed.

Add the flour, coconut, baking powder and salt and beat for 30 seconds on medium speed. Pour in the elderflower cordial and milk and mix for a further 30 seconds.

Divide the batter evenly between the two tins and bake on the middle shelf of the oven for 17–20 minutes. If the cake starts to brown quickly, cover it with foil and continue baking. The cake may appear to be soft to the touch, so insert a skewer to check if it is cooked. The skewer should come out clean.

Once cooked, remove from the oven and allow the cakes to cool in the tins for about 10 minutes, then turn out on to a wire rack to cool fully before icing.

ELDERFLOWER BUTTERCREAM ICING

Makes enough for one large 20cm cake

170g unsalted butter, at room temperature
435g icing sugar
75ml elderflower cordial
white sugar flowers, to decorate (optional)

Place the butter in a bowl and sift the icing sugar over it. Pour in the elderflower cordial and beat well with an electric hand beater until combined.

To assemble the cake, put one layer of the sponge on a serving plate and ice it with half the buttercream icing. Place the other layer on top and ice the top of the cake with the remainder of the icing. You could use some simple white sugar flowers to decorate if desired.

ETON MESS CUPCAKES

Makes 12 cupcakes

FOR THE CUPCAKES

225g unsalted butter, at
    room temperature
225g golden caster sugar
4 large eggs, free-range or
    organic
1 teaspoon vanilla extract
210g self-raising flour
25g cornflour
1 teaspoon baking powder
125g fresh or frozen
    raspberries, defrosted

FOR THE MASCARPONE FILLING

250g mascarpone
2 tablespoons icing sugar
1 teaspoon good-quality
    vanilla extract
12 fresh and ripe raspberries

These summery cupcakes were created by our chef Laura and would be welcome at any picnic or summer afternoon tea.

Preheat the oven to 180°C/160°C (fan)/350°F/gas 4. Line a 12-hole muffin tray with muffin cases.

Cream together the butter and sugar in a bowl until the mixture is light and fluffy, then add the eggs and vanilla and mix until well combined.

Add the flours and baking powder in stages, beating well after each addition. Loosely fold through the raspberries until they are equally spread through the mixture – don't worry if they break up a little.

Divide the mixture evenly between the muffin cases and bake for about 20 minutes, or until springy to touch and lightly golden. The cupcakes should still be moist.

Remove from the oven and allow them to cool in the tray for 10 minutes, then put on a wire rack to cool completely.

Make the filling by mixing together the mascarpone, icing sugar and vanilla in a bowl, using a spatula.

Using a teaspoon, scoop out the top of each cupcake to make a small hole. Spoon a generous teaspoon of the mascarpone filling into each cupcake, then press a raspberry on top, getting it as level as you can with the top of the cupcake sponge. Finish with the raspberry cream topping (see page 77).

RASPBERRY CREAM TOPPING

Makes enough for 12 regular cupcakes

425ml double cream
2½ tablespoons icing sugar
100g fresh raspberries
1 teaspoon lemon juice
crushed meringues

FOR THE MERINGUE
1 egg white
60g sugar

Whip together the cream and icing sugar until quite stiff.

Using a food processor, blend the raspberries and lemon juice to form a pulp. Sieve to remove the seeds.

Mix the raspberry pulp with the cream until well combined. Be careful not to overmix or the cream may split. Spread the cream over the cupcakes and decorate with pieces of crushed meringue.

To make the meringue, preheat the oven to 110°C/100°fan/ 225°F/¼ gas and line a baking tray with parchment paper.

Using an electric whisk, mix the egg white to stiff peaks, then add the sugar, one tablespoon at a time. Continue whisking until you have a glossy and firm meringue. Spread over the baking tray. As the meringue will be broken up, the shape is not important. Bake on the bottom shelf of the oven for about an hour, until the meringue is dry. Allow to cool, then break into pieces and sprinkle over your cupcakes.

ROCKY ROAD CUPCAKES

These make great picnic food, easy to transport and perfect for all ages. This recipe has been developed by our chef Julia and is very popular in the bakery. You could mix other chopped-up chocolate bars, such as Maltesers® or Crunchies®, through the mixture for a tasty alternative.

Makes 12 regular cupcakes

125g unsalted butter
300g dark chocolate, broken into small pieces
3 tablespoons golden syrup
200g rich tea biscuits
100g mini marshmallows, plus extra for decorating
100g dried sour cherries
100g white chocolate chips, plus 50g for the drizzle topping
100g macadamia nuts (optional)

Line a 12-hole muffin tray with muffin cases.

Heat the butter, chocolate and golden syrup in a heatproof bowl set over a pan of simmering water over a low heat until just melted. Allow to cool for about 5 minutes.

Crush the biscuits into small chunks with a rolling pin, then mix the biscuit pieces, marshmallows, cherries and white chocolate chips with the melted chocolate mixture so it is all well combined.

Divide the mixture evenly between the muffin cases and top with a handful of mini marshmallows and macadamia nuts, if using. (At Easter we top with mini eggs, which makes a delicious alternative.) Allow to set for at least 1 hour in the fridge.

Once the cupcakes are set, carefully melt the white chocolate for the drizzle topping in a heatproof bowl over a saucepan of simmering water. Using a wooden spoon, drizzle a small amount over each cupcake.

These cupcakes can be stored in airtight containers for up to 3 days at room temperature. Do not refrigerate.

CHOCOLATE FLAPJACKS

This extremely simple recipe can be made the night before you need it and will also keep very well if stored in an airtight container.

Makes one 33 x 22cm rectangle, which can be cut into 12–15 pieces as desired

525g unsalted butter
525g light brown sugar
4½ tablespoons golden syrup
675g rolled oats
9 tablespoons cocoa powder

Grease and line a 33 x 22cm baking tray. Preheat the oven to 150°C/130° (fan)/300F°/gas mark 2.

Melt the butter, sugar and golden syrup together in a pan over a gentle heat. Remove from the heat and fold in the oats and cocoa powder. Carefully pour the mixture into the tin and even the surface.

Bake in the centre of the oven for approximately 40 minutes, until bubbles have formed on the surface. Remove from the oven and allow to cool in the tray. Cover with a tea towel and leave to set fully overnight.

When you are ready to serve, cut into the desired number of squares.

ORANGE AND COCONUT SLICE

This is a recipe that Lisa's mother Marlene used to make for her and her brother as children. It is so easy and quick, it just needs refrigeration time, as we all agree that it tastes best eaten chilled. If the weather is hot, it might even be best putting it in the freezer for an hour before packing your picnic, especially if your picnic spot is some distance from home.

Makes one 33 x 22cm rectangle, which can be cut into 12–15 pieces as desired

FOR THE BASE

230g unsalted butter
1 x 397g tin condensed milk
250g desiccated coconut
400g rich tea biscuits (approximately 2 packets)
juice and grated zest of 1 orange

FOR THE ICING

30g unsalted butter, at room temperature
275g icing sugar
1 teaspoon water
juice of 1 orange

Grease a 33 x 22cm baking tray.

Melt the butter and condensed milk in a pan over a low heat. Put the biscuits into a sealed plastic bag and crush them with a rolling pin.

In a bowl, combine the coconut, biscuits, orange juice and zest with the butter and condensed milk. Spread the mixture out in the baking tray and press down evenly so that the base of the tray is well covered and the surface is smooth. Put in the fridge to cool before icing.

To make the icing, beat all the ingredients, except the orange juice, together with an electric hand beater. Add the juice a little at a time to achieve the desired consistency. You may need to add a little more icing sugar.

When the base is cold, pour the icing over the top and return the tray to the fridge. Once set, cut it into the desired number of pieces and serve.

LIME AND COCONUT MACAROONS

These English-style macaroons have a light and fresh flavour that is inspired by our best-selling lime and coconut cupcakes. Ideally they should be eaten on the day they are made, as they have a tendency to become soft if kept for too long. Store any you don't eat in an airtight container for no more than a couple of days.

Makes 20 macaroons

200g desiccated coconut
200g condensed milk
zest of 1 lime
2 egg whites
¼ teaspoon salt
30g golden caster sugar

Preheat the oven to 180°C/160°C (fan)/350°F/gas 4. Line a baking tray with parchment paper and set aside.

Combine the coconut, condensed milk and lime zest in a bowl, mix thoroughly and set aside.

Put the egg whites into a medium-sized bowl with the salt. Beat with an electric beater until the whites are frothy. Add the sugar and continue beating until shiny and stiff peaks are formed. Fold the meringue into the coconut mixture with a metal spoon until just combined.

Drop heaped tablespoons of the mixture onto the baking tray, keeping a 4cm space between each macaroon. The mixture must be spooned out immediately or it will start weeping.

Bake for 15–20 minutes, or until golden brown. Remove from the oven and leave to cool on the tray for 10 minutes before transferring to wire racks to cool completely.

COURGETTE AND GINGER LOAF

This delicious, moist, dairy-free loaf was created by our chef Lisa Chan and it is always popular in our shops. It is ideal for picnics because it keeps well and is easy to transport, simply wrapped in foil.

Makes one 900g loaf, to cut into 8–10 slices

160g plain flour
1½ teaspoons ground cinnamon
½ teaspoon ground ginger
½ teaspoon nutmeg
½ teaspoon salt
½ teaspoon baking powder
½ teaspoon bicarbonate of soda
110g soft brown sugar
100g golden caster sugar
125ml vegetable oil
150g apple sauce
2 pieces of stem ginger, chopped
2 large free-range or organic eggs
1 courgette (approximately 150–200g), grated

Preheat the oven to 190°C/170° (fan)/375°F/gas mark 5. Grease and line a 900g loaf tin with greaseproof paper or a loaf tin liner.

Place the flour, spices, salt, baking powder and bicarbonate of soda in a bowl and stir to combine.

In a separate bowl mix together the sugars, oil, apple sauce, stem ginger and eggs with a wooden spoon. Then pour this mixture into the flour mixture and stir again until just combined. Fold in the grated courgette.

Pour the batter into the prepared tin and bake in the oven for 30–40 minutes, until a skewer comes out clean. It will be golden brown in colour. Remove from the oven and allow to cool in the tin.

SUMMER SAVOURY MUFFINS

This muffin recipe was inspired by Lisa's sister-in-law, Kerrin, an excellent cook who lives in Sydney, Australia. She suggested using her walnut pesto for the base, adding lemon zest to the herbs and walnuts to give it the taste of summer we wanted for our picnic food. Thanks, Kerrin!

Makes 18 muffins

FOR THE PESTO
50g walnuts
25g fresh basil, roughly chopped
25g fresh mint, roughly chopped
15g fresh parsley, roughly chopped
1 garlic clove
zest of ½ lemon
1 teaspoon salt
¼ teaspoon ground black pepper
100ml olive oil

FOR THE MUFFIN BATTER
500g self-raising flour
1 teaspoon salt
1 teaspoon ground black pepper
100g unsalted butter
400ml milk
40 ml olive oil
2 eggs
250g feta, cut into 1.5cm cubes
170g walnuts, roughly chopped

Preheat the oven to 180°C/160°C (fan)/350°F/gas 4. Line a baking tray with baking parchment and two muffin trays with muffin cases.

Make the pesto first. Place the walnuts on the baking tray and bake for 15–20 minutes. Remove, set aside to cool slightly, then transfer to a food processor with the basil, mint, parsley, garlic, lemon zest, salt and pepper. Blend for 30 seconds or until all the ingredients are combined, adding the olive oil in a slow stream while the food processor is blending. Scrape down the sides, then blend for a final 30 seconds. Transfer to a bowl and set aside.

To make the muffins, first put the flour, salt, and black pepper into a medium bowl.

Place a heatproof bowl over a pan of simmering water and melt the butter. Remove from the heat and set aside.

Make a well in the centre of the flour and pour the milk and oil into it. Add the eggs and whisk together, then pour in the melted butter and beat until just combined. With a rubber spatula, fold through 120g of the pesto and the cubed feta.

Spoon the mixture into the muffin cases, filling each one about two-thirds full. Spoon ½ teaspoon of the remaining pesto on top of each muffin and roughly swirl it through the mix with the end of the spoon. Sprinkle the chopped walnuts evenly across all the muffins and press them in gently.

Bake in the oven for 13–15 minutes, or until a skewer comes out clean. Remove from the oven and leave to cool in the trays for 10 minutes, before removing them to a wire rack to cool completely. These muffins would be delicious served slightly warm or at room temperature.

CLUB SANDWICHES

Lisa's mother Marlene donated this amazing recipe proving once again that the food from Lisa's childhood in New Zealand and Australia makes ideal picnic fare.

Makes one serving, so multiply depending on how many you need

salted butter, at room temperature
4 slices of fresh white bread
a slice or two of ham
Dijon mustard
1 sliced tomato
salt and pepper
1 hard-boiled egg, mashed with mayonnaise and chives

Butter a slice of bread, top with a slice of ham and spread with Dijon mustard. Butter the second slice of bread and place it on top of the mustardy ham, then butter the top side of the bread, cover with the sliced tomato and season with salt and pepper. Butter the third slice of bread, place on the tomato, then butter the top side and spread the egg mixture evenly over it. Finally, butter the fourth slice of bread on one side only and lay it on top of the egg mixture.

Trim the crusts of the sandwich and cut carefully into three fingers.

Baby Shower

Baby showers are commonly thought of as an American custom, but in our years of running Primrose Bakery we have seen a huge increase in their popularity in the UK. They are usually organized by a close friend of the mother-to-be and are a lovely way of getting together with friends and family before the baby is born, both to celebrate the impending arrival and also to enjoy a peaceful occasion before all the hard work (and pleasure, of course) a new baby will bring.

We make lots of baby-themed cupcakes at the bakery and are lucky enough to have a huge range of very cute sugar and plastic cake decorations, both for baby showers and to celebrate new arrivals.

For this chapter, however, we wanted to explore all aspects of the baby shower and think about the kind of food it would be nice to serve at one. We've gone for a Moroccan theme that complements the flavours we've chosen and gives a slightly different take on a more traditional tea. We chose the beautiful Moroccan courtyard at the Rococo chocolate shop in Belgravia in London as the setting for our pictures. This small garden is open to customers and a charming place in which to enjoy their delicious chocolates with a cup of tea.

Lemon and Rose Layer Cake

Makes one 3-layer 20cm cake

340g golden caster sugar
315g self-raising flour
40g cornflour
1½ teaspoons baking powder
6 large eggs, preferably
 free-range or organic
340g unsalted butter,
 at room temperature
4 tablespoons milk
zest of 3 lemons

The combination of lemon and rose flavours in this pretty three-tiered cake makes it a beautiful and delicious centrepiece.

Preheat the oven to 180°C/160°C (fan)/350°F/gas 4. Grease and line three 20cm sandwich baking tins.

Put the dry ingredients into a food processor and pulse to combine. Add the eggs, butter, milk and lemon zest and pulse for a further 8 seconds. Remove the lid and scrape down the sides with a spatula to make sure all the ingredients are well combined. Pulse again for approximately 5 seconds. Divide the batter evenly between the three tins and even out with a flat knife.

Bake in the oven for 18–20 minutes. If possible, put all three tins on the middle shelf. If not, it is a good idea to rotate the tins between the shelves while cooking.

Check that all the cakes are cooked by inserting a skewer into the centre of each one. It should come out clean. The tops of the sponges should be golden brown and springy to the touch. Remove from the oven and leave to cool in the tins for 10 minutes before turning out to cool fully on a wire rack.

Rose Petal Icing

600ml double cream
approximately ½ teaspoon
 rose water (we like the
 Star Kay White brand)
rose petal jam
Turkish delight, to decorate
a few drops of pink food
 colouring (optional)

To prepare the icing, whip the cream and rose water with an electric hand beater to form soft peaks, being very careful not to overbeat. Check the taste, as the strength of rose water varies from brand to brand, and you may need to add a bit more. For pink icing, add a few drops of pink food colouring.

To assemble the cake, place one layer on a serving plate and spread first with a thin layer of rose petal jam, then with a thin layer of the cream. Put the second layer of cake on top and repeat the process. Put the final cake layer on top, then, using the remaining cream, cover the top of the cake. (If you want to ice the sides of the cake, just make sure you haven't used too much jam in the layers so that it comes out at the sides of the cake. It will be easier to spread the cream around the sides if it doesn't.).

We've decorated our cake with pieces of Turkish delight, but sugared or real rose petals or pomegranate seeds would work just as well.

Orange, Pistachio and Almond Cake

This gluten-free cake has taken many attempts to get absolutely right, but we feel we have now created a fantastic recipe that will be greeted with delight at any baby shower or afternoon tea.

Makes one single-layer 23cm cake

FOR THE CARAMEL SAUCE
3 oranges
2 tablespoons water
100g granulated sugar
60g unsalted butter

FOR THE CAKE
200g unsalted butter, at room temperature
200g caster sugar
3 large eggs, preferably free-range or organic
juice of 3 oranges
2 teaspoons orange blossom essence
100g gluten-free plain flour
1 teaspoon gluten-free baking powder
2 teaspoons ground cardamom
½ teaspoon salt
160g fine instant polenta
200g ground almonds
2 tablespoons good-quality marmalade
1 tablespoon water
40g chopped, unsalted pistachios

Grease and line a 23cm baking tin, then place this inside a larger tin or tray to protect your oven from any drips. Preheat the oven to 180°C/160°C (fan)/350°F/gas 4.

First make the caramel sauce. Finely zest the oranges and reserve for later. Using a serrated knife, carefully slice off the top and bottom of each orange and then the sides, following the shape of the orange. Slice the peeled orange horizontally into roughly 0.5cm thick pieces, depending on the size of the orange.

In a heavy-based pan off the heat, place the water and sugar for the caramel and mix a little until you have a paste-like consistency. Transfer to a medium to high heat, but do not stir, as this will incorporate air into the caramel and cause it to crystallize.

Keep heating the sugar until it is light brown in colour. Remove from the heat and carefully add the butter, a little at a time. Be very careful to hold the pan away from you, as it can easily spatter.

Once all the butter is incorporated, quickly pour the caramel into the prepared tin and leave to cool slightly. Then lay the orange slices neatly on top.

Now make the sponge. Cream the butter and sugar together, then add the eggs, one by one, followed by the orange juice, orange blossom essence and reserved zest. Mix until well combined. Sift the flour, baking powder, cardamom and salt together in a bowl, then add to the batter along with the polenta and ground almonds. Pour this batter into the tin on top of the oranges and caramel and spread evenly.

Bake in the oven for about 40 minutes, until springy to touch or when an inserted skewer comes out clean. Be careful not to overbake. Remove from the oven and leave to cool in the tin for about 5 minutes, then turn upside down onto a cake board or plate so that the orange slices are now on the top. Remove the layer of baking paper at this point. Allow to cool fully.

Once cool, melt the marmalade and water together in a small pan and brush over the surface of the cake to give it a shiny appearance. Top with the chopped pistachios.

Date Bars

Keeping to the North African theme of our baby shower, these date bars are an excellent source of fibre, nutrients and vitamins as well as a tempting treat.

Makes one 23cm square, to be cut into the desired number of pieces

180g rolled oats
260g plain flour, sifted
¼ teaspoon salt
270g soft brown sugar
1 teaspoon bicarbonate of soda
280g unsalted butter, softened
30g roughly chopped raw almonds

FOR THE FILLING
425g pitted dates, diced
310ml water
90g soft brown sugar
1¼ teaspoons freshly squeezed lemon juice
   (about half a lemon's worth)

Preheat the oven to 170°C/155°C (fan)/325°F/gas 3. Grease and line a 23cm square baking tray.

In a large bowl, combine the oats, flour, salt, sugar and bicarbonate of soda. Add the butter and mix until crumbly. Press half the mixture into the bottom of the prepared tray.

In a small pan over a medium heat, combine the dates, water and brown sugar. Bring to the boil and cook until thickened. Stir in the lemon juice and remove from the heat. Spread the filling evenly over the base, then pat the remaining crumb mixture over the top. Sprinkle with the chopped almonds.

Bake in the oven for 20–25 minutes, or until the top is lightly toasted. Remove from the oven and allow to cool fully before cutting into the desired number of pieces.

Rose and Violet Mini Chocolate Bombs

Makes 48 mini cupcakes

**115g good-quality dark
  chocolate (at least 70%
  cocoa solids if possible)**
**85g unsalted butter, at
  room temperature**
175g soft brown sugar
2 large eggs, separated
185g plain flour
¾ teaspoon baking powder
**¾ teaspoon bicarbonate
  of soda**
pinch of salt
**250ml semi-skimmed milk,
  at room temperature**
**1 teaspoon good-quality
  vanilla extract**

We think of these as the 'skinny' version of our chocolate bomb cupcakes (see page 188). Their pretty pink and lilac colours and delicate flavour fit perfectly at the tea table or would make a lovely gift for the expectant mother. You could also make them as regular cupcakes.

Preheat the oven to 190°C/170°C (fan)/375°F/gas 5. Line a mini-cupcake tray with muffin cases.

Break the dark chocolate into small pieces and melt, either in the microwave on a medium heat at 10–20 second intervals, stirring well in between, or in a heatproof bowl over a pan of simmering water on the hob, making sure the bowl doesn't touch the water. Be careful not to burn the chocolate. Remove from the heat and leave to cool slightly.

Cream the butter and sugar together using an electric hand beater until pale and smooth. In a separate bowl and with clean beaters beat the egg yolks for several minutes. Slowly add the egg yolks to the creamed butter and sugar and beat well. Beat in the melted chocolate.

In a separate bowl combine the flour, baking powder, bicarbonate of soda and salt. Combine the milk and vanilla in a jug. Add the flour mixture to the chocolate, butter and sugar in stages, alternating with the milk and vanilla. Beat very well after each addition.

In a clean bowl, whisk the egg whites until soft peaks start to form. Carefully fold the egg whites into the main batter using a metal spoon. Do not beat or you will take all the air out of the cake.

Spoon the mixture equally into the muffin cases until they are about two-thirds full. The batter will be of a fairly liquid consistency, so take care when spooning it out – it can end up being very messy! You could use a jug to pour the batter into the muffin cases if it gets too difficult to spoon.

Bake for approximately 15 minutes, then remove from the oven and leave in the tray for 10 minutes or so before transferring to wire racks to cool before finishing with Marshmallow Topping (see page 100).

These cupcakes can be stored un-iced for 3 days at room temperature in an airtight container. They are very moist, so they tend to keep very well if stored correctly.

Marshmallow Topping

350g granulated sugar
60ml water
3 large egg whites
¼ teaspoon cream of tartar
1 teaspoon rose water (we use the Star Kay White brand)
a few drops of pink food colouring
1 teaspoon violet essence
1 teaspoon of lilac food colouring (we used Le Jardin d'Elen
** 'Sirop a la Violette')**
crystallized rose or violet petals, to decorate

Fill a medium pan with water to a depth of approximately
2cm and place it over a low heat. Make sure the water in the pan
is not boiling, otherwise the bottom of the mixture will start to
cook, resulting in small particles throughout the marshmallow; it
should be barely simmering, with steam coming from the top and
only a few bubbles.

Place the sugar, water, egg whites and cream of tartar in a
medium to large heatproof bowl. Using an electric hand beater,
beat the mixture for 1 minute on high speed until it is opaque,
white and foamy.

Place the bowl over the pan of water. Immediately continue
beating with the hand-held beater on a high speed for a further
12–13 minutes, ensuring that the water in the saucepan remains
at a gentle simmer. If it does start boiling, turn down the heat and
add a little cold water to the pan.

After 12–13 minutes, the mixture should form stiff peaks that
stand straight up when the beaters are stopped and removed.

Remove the bowl from the heat and divide the marshmallow
mixture into two bowls. Add the rose water to one bowl with
a drop of pink food colouring and continue beating on high speed
for a further 2 minutes. Add the violet essence to the second bowl
with a drop of lilac food colouring and do the same. During this
time, the mixtures will thicken further and become shinier.

When you are ready to ice the cakes, spoon one of the icings
into a large piping bag with a large round piping tip (or cut off
the tip so there is approximately a 1cm circle when piped). Pipe
a spiral of icing approximately 5cm high onto each cupcake to
make a cone-shaped mound. Continue to ice half the cakes and
then repeat with the second bowl of icing.

Decorate with either rose or violet petals.

Rose and Pistachio Mini Meringues

Makes approximately
20 finished meringues

FOR THE MERINGUES

2 egg whites
120g caster sugar
¾ teaspoon rose water
**3–4 drops of pink food
    colouring (optional)**
**15g unsalted shelled
    pistachios, chopped into
    very fine pieces**

FOR THE CREAM FILLING

**200ml double or whipping
    cream**
1 tablespoon icing sugar
2 tablespoons rose syrup
1 teaspoon rose essence

*Our chef Laura is a big fan of anything rose-scented (making her
very popular with Lisa!), and her pretty, tiny meringues are both
delicious to taste and beautiful to look at.*

Preheat the oven to 110°C/90°C (fan)/225°F/gas ¼. Line a
baking tray with parchment paper.

Whisk the egg whites with an electric hand beater until they
reach stiff peaks. Add the sugar 1 tablespoon at a time, allowing
it to dissolve before each new addition. Once all the sugar has
been incorporated, gently fold in the rose water, and food colouring, if using, being careful not to overmix the meringue.

Put a round-tipped nozzle into a piping bag and fill with the
meringue. Pipe the meringue into 4cm circles on the lined baking
tray, lifting the nozzle to finish, creating a peak shape. Sprinkle
over the chopped pistachios.

Bake in the oven for about 1 hour and 20 minutes, or until dry.
The meringues are ready when you are able to lift them cleanly
from the baking tray. They should still be slightly chewy inside.
Remove from the oven and allow them to cool completely on wire
racks.

To make the filling, whip the cream with the icing sugar until
stiff. Gently fold in the rose syrup and essence.

Carefully pipe or spoon a small amount of the cream onto the
underside of one meringue, then sandwich together with a second
meringue of equal size and leave to set. Repeat until all meringues
are sandwiched together.

Ned's Orange and Cinnamon Fruit Salad

Lisa's son Ned came home from school one day with some recipe books and was keen to do some cooking with her. We always have a lot of oranges left at the bakery, as we use much more rind than juice, so Lisa took some home and together they came up with this delicious and healthy fruit salad. The fact that Ned could use a sharp knife to cut the oranges added greatly to its appeal for him.

Makes 4–6 servings

4 large oranges
4 teaspoons cinnamon sugar
   (either ready-made or home-made)

Peel the oranges carefully with a sharp knife, removing all the skin and pith but keeping as much flesh as possible. Slice into 0.5cm rounds and lay out on a large flat plate.

   To make your own cinnamon sugar, grind cinnamon sticks in a grinder to make a powder, then stir this through some caster sugar. Sprinkle the oranges with the cinnamon sugar, covering each slice, and refrigerate for at least 2 hours before serving.

Pomegranate Ice Cubes

These ice cubes could be used in our home-made lemonades (opposite), or would look really pretty simply dropped into sparkling water. You'll need some ice cube trays.

water
pomegranate syrup (we use the Monin brand)
pomegranate seeds (super-markets sell ready-prepared seeds, or simply cut a few pomegranates in half and knock out the seeds with a wooden spoon into a bowl or dish)

Fill a 2-litre measuring jug about two-thirds full with water, add a little pomegranate syrup to give colour, and stir in the seeds. Pour into the desired number of ice cube trays, making sure the seeds are evenly distributed through the trays.

Put into the freezer overnight or for at least a few hours, to freeze completely.

Home-made Lemonade

A fresh and colourful drink to serve at the baby shower tea, home-made lemonade can be made in a number of different flavours. Here are three suggestions.

PINK LEMONADE

There are a couple of variations here, the first American in flavour, the second more traditionally British.

VERSION 1
300g caster sugar
1 litre water
235ml cranberry juice
235ml lemon juice, freshly squeezed if possible
ice

Make a syrup by dissolving the sugar with 250ml of the water in a pan over a low heat. Remove from the heat, then add the remaining 750ml of water and the cranberry and lemon juice. Check for taste. Allow to cool for at least an hour, then serve with ice.

VERSION 2
300g caster sugar
juice of 1–2 lemons
juice of 1 orange
3 x 150g punnets of raspberries
350ml water
ice
sparkling water
fresh mint leaves, to garnish

Make a syrup by heating the sugar, lemon and orange juice, raspberries and water in a pan. Bring to the boil, stirring constantly, then leave to cool. Pour the mixture through a sieve and press down with a spoon to extract all the juice. To serve, pour a small amount of syrup into a glass with lots of ice and dilute with sparkling water. Garnish with fresh mint leaves and serve.

MINT LEMONADE

450g caster sugar
1.5 litres water
470ml fresh lemon juice
a large handful of fresh mint leaves
ice

Make a syrup by putting the sugar and 500ml of the water into a pan and bringing to the boil. Keep stirring until the sugar is dissolved, then remove from the heat and allow to cool. Put the lemon juice into a large jug filled with ice. Add the remaining litre of water and the syrup, checking for taste. Stir in most of the mint leaves and allow to chill in the fridge for at least an hour. To serve, pour into glasses with ice and garnish with a few extra fresh mint leaves.

POMEGRANATE LEMONADE

90g caster sugar
115ml lemon juice
ice
470ml pomegranate juice
1.2 litres water
fresh mint leaves, to garnish

Make a syrup by dissolving the sugar and lemon juice in a small pan over a low heat and stirring until fully dissolved. Pour the syrup into a large jug filled with ice, add the pomegranate juice, stir well to combine, then add the water and stir again. Serve in glasses filled with ice and garnish with fresh mint leaves.

Finishing Touches

MINT TEA

Put plenty of fresh mint leaves into a teapot, fill with boiling water, leave for a few minutes, then serve in china cups or glasses, with or without sugar.

PITTA BREAD AND HUMMUS

A simple and delicious dish to serve at tea, this is actually one of our favourite things to eat after all the cakes and biscuits we spend our days surrounded by in the bakery! Overdosing on sugar makes us crave something salty and savoury and hummus is ideal. Serve with wholemeal or plain pitta bread, lightly toasted and cut in half.

BAKLAVA

This is filo pastry filled with layers of chopped nuts and honey or syrup. It is very rich and sweet but would fit in well with our theme. In the Dalston area of London there are some amazing shops where you can buy authentic baklava in different shapes and slightly varying flavours. Selfridges food hall also sells a very good selection.

TURKISH DELIGHT

Like baklava, Turkish delight is a very sweet mixture of starch and sugar. Flavoured with a wide variety of ingredients such as pistachios, hazelnuts, rose water or lemon and dusted with icing sugar, it's certainly not to everyone's taste, but for those who love it, it's fairly easy to find in the supermarket or specialist food shops.

Afternoon Tea Party

One of the reasons we started Primrose Bakery was our shared love of afternoon tea, and we spent many happy afternoons trying out tea in different places all over London and anywhere else we visited in the UK or abroad. Although we don't serve a classic afternoon tea in the bakery, we felt we couldn't leave it out of this book, as there is probably no nicer occasion to enjoy with family and friends, either at home or in a hotel or tea room.

To make our tea a bit special, we decided it would have a Japanese theme. In October 2011, Primrose Bakery were invited to a British fair being held in Hankyu, a big department store in Osaka, Japan. It was an amazing opportunity – and one we couldn't refuse – so we went to Japan for ten days and took our chef Julia and manager Faye with us to help.

We sold 2,500 mini cupcakes every day, packaged in boxes of five, which all had to look exactly the same. We were given only twenty-four hours to train a Japanese pastry chef to assist us, which proved almost impossible, though certainly not from any lack of hard work and effort on his part. The whole experience was exhausting but extremely rewarding, and we were privileged to meet a great many amazing Japanese people during our stay.

The recipes in this chapter have been inspired by our trip to Japan and by some of the food and drink we enjoyed while we were there.

Jasmine Cake

This recipe started out as cupcakes and evolved into a layer cake. The fragrant, moist sponge makes it perfect for afternoon tea.

Makes one 20cm layer cake

180ml milk
2 teaspoons loose-leaf jasmine tea
250g self-raising flour
½ teaspoon baking powder
¼ teaspoon salt
250g unsalted butter, at room temperature
250g golden caster sugar
3 large eggs, preferably free-range or organic
**1 teaspoon jasmine essence (you should find this in
  an Asian grocery store or online)**

Preheat the oven to 180°C/160°C (fan)/350°F/gas 4. Grease and line two 20cm sandwich baking tins.

Heat the milk in a pan on the hob until it boils (watch it closely, as it can quickly boil over). Add the jasmine tea leaves to the hot milk, pour into a heatproof bowl, cover with clingfilm and set aside until cool. Once cool, drain the tea leaves by pouring the milk through a sieve. Discard the tea leaves.

Sift the flour, baking powder and salt into a separate bowl and set aside.

Cream the butter and sugar in another bowl until light and fluffy. Add the eggs, one at a time, ensuring each one is well incorporated before adding the next. Add the jasmine essence with the last egg.

Add one-third of the flour and beat with an electric hand beater on a low speed until combined. Pour in one-third of the jasmine tea milk and beat again on a low speed until combined. Continue to add the flour and milk, alternating until all has been incorporated.

Divide the batter evenly between the two tins and bake in the oven for 20–25 minutes, or until a skewer comes out clean.

Remove from the oven and leave to cool in the tins for about 10 minutes, then turn out onto a wire rack to cool completely.

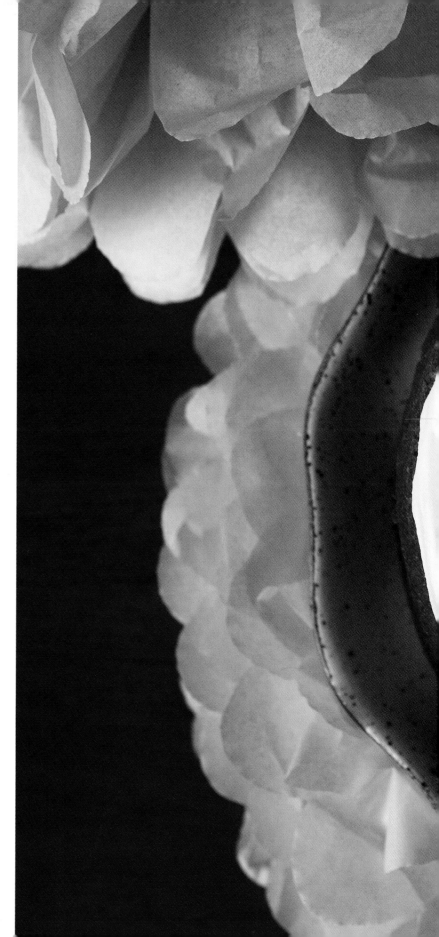

Jasmine and Vanilla Buttercream Icing

100g unsalted butter
50ml milk
1 teaspoon vanilla extract
¼ teaspoon jasmine essence
500g icing sugar, sifted

Put the butter, milk, vanilla, jasmine essence and half the icing sugar into a bowl and beat with an electric hand beater on a low speed until well combined. Add the remaining icing sugar and beat again on a low speed until thoroughly combined and of a smooth and creamy consistency.

Put one layer of sponge on a cake plate and spread a layer of icing over the top of it, then put the other layer on top and use the rest of the icing to ice the top of the cake. Either leave undecorated or use some sugar or fresh flowers to make a beautiful centrepiece.

Mini Cherry Blossom Cupcakes

Cherry blossom is so closely associated with Japan that we really wanted to incorporate cherries into our afternoon tea. We think these mini cupcakes work really well, particularly with the added extra of some cherry brandy!

Makes 12 mini cupcakes

30g dried sour cherries
50ml cherry brandy
50g unsalted butter, at room temperature
50g caster sugar, preferably golden
1 large egg, preferably free-range or organic
50g self-raising flour

Preheat the oven to 180°C/160°C (fan)/350°F/gas 4. Line a 12-hole mini muffin tray with mini muffin cases.

Soak the cherries in the brandy for at least one hour before you start.

In a large bowl, cream together the butter and sugar until pale and fluffy. Add the egg, mix well, then add the flour and beat until all is combined.

Drain the cherries from the brandy, reserving the brandy for the icing.

Divide the mixture evenly between the muffin cases and add 2 cherries to each case. Bake in the oven for approximately 15 minutes, or until an inserted skewer comes out clean. Remove from the oven and allow the cakes to cool in the tray for 10 minutes or so before turning out onto a wire rack to cool completely.

Cherry Buttercream Icing

50g unsalted butter, at room temperature
250g icing sugar
50ml cherry brandy (reserved from soaking the cherries for the sponge, see above)
dried sour cherries, to decorate

Put the butter and icing sugar into a bowl and beat with an electric hand beater on a low speed until smooth. Add the cherry brandy and beat again until well combined.

Ice each cupcake with some of this icing, decorate with a couple of cherries and serve.

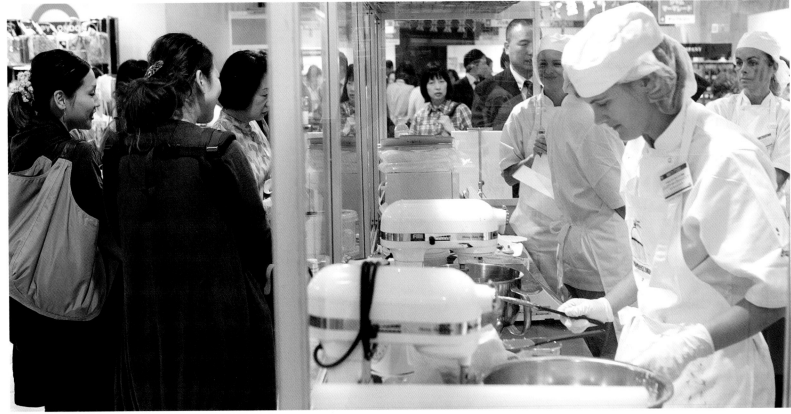

Sake Macaroons

No Japanese tea would be complete without sake and we found it works perfectly as a flavouring for macaroons. Macaroons look like they would be difficult to make at home, but with our chef Laura's recipe, these should be easy to recreate.

Makes about 24 macaroons

135g ground almonds
125g icing sugar
3 large egg whites
100g granulated sugar
1 tablespoon egg white
a few drops of purple or lilac food colouring

Preheat the oven to 140°C/120° (fan)/275°F/gas 1 and line two baking trays with parchment paper. To help you when you come to pipe the shell mixture onto the paper, draw outlines round a £2 coin with a pencil, leaving 2cm between each one.

Using a food processor, mix the ground almonds and icing sugar together to get the ingredients as fine as possible.

In a clean, dry bowl, whisk the 3 egg whites with an electric hand beater until they reach stiff peaks. Add the granulated sugar, a tablespoonful at a time, whisking continuously. Once all the sugar has been added, continue to whisk for about a minute to allow the sugar to completely dissolve. The mixture should by then be stiff and glossy.

Using a spatula, gently fold in the ground almond and icing sugar mixture. Fold until just combined – the mixture should still be quite stiff. Now add the tablespoon of unwhisked egg white and a few drops of purple or lilac food colouring to the mixture, which will help to loosen the consistency of the macaroon. Fold through the mixture until you have the desired colour and the mixture is shiny.

If possible, use a piping bag with a 1cm round nozzle. You can spoon the mixture instead, if you like, but a piping bag will give a neater result. Spoon the mixture into the piping bag and pipe rounds using the guide you have drawn on the parchment paper, ensuring you leave space in between as they will expand when baked. Allow the shells to sit for about an hour before baking. This is very important, to avoid cracking. You want the macaroon to form a 'skin'.

Bake in the oven for 12–16 minutes. When cooked you should be able to lift each shell cleanly off the tray. Allow to cool on the trays.

Sake Ganache Filling

175g white chocolate
40g double cream
50g sake

To make the ganache filling, warm the white chocolate in a bowl either in the microwave on a medium heat at 10–20 second intervals, stirring well in between or in a heatproof bowl over a pan of simmering water on the hob, making sure the bowl doesn't touch the water. It doesn't need to be completely melted but it will be easier to use if slightly warm. Bring the cream to a boil in a pan and pour over the warmed chocolate, mixing with a wooden spoon until smooth and glossy. Add the sake and mix again. Allow the mixture to cool.

Once the macaroon shells are cool, turn half of them over. Either with a piping bag or a spoon, place a teaspoon of the cooled ganache filling on the flat side of each shell and sandwich together with the rest of the macaroons.

Store in an airtight container in the fridge, and ideally allow the macaroons to reach room temperature before serving. They will keep in the fridge for 2 or 3 days.

Plum Wine Macaroons

A variation on the sake macaroons and another excuse to use our favourite plum wine, the peachy colour of these would look lovely on a plate mixed with the lilac sake macaroons (see page 120).

Makes about 24 macaroons

135g ground almonds
125g icing sugar
3 large egg whites
100g granulated sugar
1 tablespoon egg white
a few drops of orange food colouring

To make the macaroon shells, follow the method for Sake Macaroons (see page 120), substituting orange food colouring for lilac.

Plum Wine Filling

60g butter, at room temperature or slightly softened
225g icing sugar
40ml plum wine
plum jam

Beat the butter and icing sugar together and add the plum wine. Taste and if necessary add a little more plum wine, depending on how strong you would like the filling to be.

To assemble the macaroons, sandwich 2 shells with a teaspoon of plum wine filling and a pea-sized drop of plum jam.

Store in an airtight container in the fridge, and ideally allow the macaroons to reach room temperature before serving. They will keep in the fridge for 2 or 3 days.

Green Tea Scones with Lemon Cream

No afternoon tea would be complete without scones, so here is a Japanese-inspired scone, developed by our chef, Laura.

Makes approximately 8 scones, about 5cm in diameter

125ml milk, plus a little for brushing
3 green tea bags
2 teaspoons lemon juice
220g self-raising flour
2 heaped teaspoons matcha (green tea) powder
a pinch of salt
50g caster sugar
50g unsalted butter, chilled

Heat the milk in a pan with the green tea bags. Take off the heat, cover and leave to infuse for about 30 minutes. Remove the tea bags and add the lemon juice.

Heat the oven to 200°C/180°C (fan)/400°F/gas 6. Line a baking tray with parchment paper.

Mix together the flour, matcha powder, salt and sugar. Cut the butter into small pieces, then, using your fingertips, mix it with the dry ingredients to create the consistency of breadcrumbs. Add the milk mixture and knead briefly into a smooth dough, being careful not to overmix.

On a flat, lightly floured surface, roll the dough out to 2.5cm thickness and cut into circles, using a circular cutter or the top of a glass. Place the scones on the baking tray and brush the tops with milk.

Bake in the oven for 10–12 minutes, until golden and well risen. Remove from the oven and allow to cool on a wire rack.

Lemon Cream

300ml double cream
1 teaspoon icing sugar
1 dessertspoon lemon curd

Make the lemon cream just before you are ready to use it. Whip the cream and icing sugar until stiff, then fold in the lemon curd.

Split the cooled scones and fill with some of the lemon cream. Serve immediately.

Scones are best eaten on the day they are made, when they are at their freshest, as they tend to go stale quite quickly.

Green Tea Marble Loaf Cake with White Chocolate Icing

Makes one 900g loaf cake, to cut into 8–10 slices

180g golden caster sugar
160ml vegetable oil
½ teaspoon vanilla extract
245g plain flour
½ teaspoon bicarbonate of soda
¼ teaspoon salt
2 large eggs, preferably free-range or organic
200ml buttermilk (or alternatively 200ml milk
plus juice of ½ lemon)
4 teaspoons powdered green tea

Preheat the oven to 180°C/160°C (fan)/350°F/gas 4. Grease a 900g loaf tin and line with parchment paper or a loaf tin liner.

Combine the sugar, oil and vanilla extract in a large bowl and beat or whisk for 3–5 minutes, using an electric hand beater.

Add the flour, bicarbonate of soda and salt and mix until well combined. Add the eggs and buttermilk and mix again thoroughly. Pour one-third of the mixture into a bowl and set aside.

Beat the powdered green tea into the remaining two-thirds of the batter and pour into the prepared loaf tin. Add the batter that was set aside, pouring it in a circular motion into the tin. Using a skewer, swirl the white batter into the green tea batter, ensuring you don't overmix.

Bake in the oven for 35–40 minutes, or until the skewer comes out clean. Remove from the oven and allow to cool fully before icing.

White Chocolate Buttercream Icing

100g white chocolate
approx 60g (4 tablespoons) cream
1 x quantity jasmine and vanilla buttercream (see page 115)
3 tablespoons double cream

Break the white chocolate into small pieces and melt, either in the microwave on a medium heat at 10–20 second intervals, stirring well in between, or in a bowl over a pan of simmering water on the hob, making sure the bowl doesn't touch the water. Be careful not to burn the chocolate. Remove from the heat and allow to cool.

Combine all the ingredients and beat well until everything comes together. It is best to use this icing immediately. If it begins to stiffen too much, soften it with a bit more double cream or warm it in the microwave for 10 seconds, beating well again before using.

Cover the top of the loaf with a generous layer of icing and serve.

Note: This icing needs to be stored in the fridge because it contains cream, and will need to be beaten well again if it has become too cold and stiff to use.

Plum Wine Drizzle Loaf

Makes one 400–450g loaf cake,
to cut into 8–10 slices

FOR THE CAKE

**50g mixed dried fruit (we
used a mixture of sultanas,
raisins, cranberries and
blueberries) (optional)**
**2 tablespoons plum wine,
plus extra to soak the
dried fruits**
**2 large eggs, preferably
free-range or organic**
80g caster sugar
90g plain flour
1 teaspoon baking powder
50g unsalted butter, melted
20g vegetable oil

FOR THE SYRUP

3 tablespoons caster sugar
50ml water
100ml plum wine
1 tablespoon lemon juice

*Our amazing Japanese shop assistant, Mariko, recommended we
make a plum wine cake, as she remembers her mother making
her one back home in Japan. We ended up making two, one with
dried fruit and one plain. Both taste better when chilled.*

Preheat the oven to 180°C/160°C (fan)/350°F/gas 4. Grease
a 900g loaf tin and line with parchment paper or a loaf tin liner.

If using dried fruit, soak it in enough plum wine to cover and
leave for at least an hour, until the fruit has swelled. Drain.

Using an electric hand beater, whisk the eggs and sugar until
pale, frothy and thick. Gently fold in the flour and baking powder,
then the 2 tablespoons of plum wine, melted butter and oil. Mix
until well combined but be careful not to knock the air out of the
mixture. Fold in the dried fruit, if using.

Pour the mixture into the loaf tin and bake in the oven for
30 minutes, until golden and springy to touch.

Just before you remove the cake from the oven, make the syrup.
Bring the sugar, water and plum wine to the boil, then add the
lemon juice. While still hot, pour all the syrup over the cake – you
might want to put the cake into a container while you do this to
avoid any drips. Pour the reserved fruit (if using) and liquid over
the top. Leave the cake to cool.

When it is cool, wrap the cake in clingfilm and refrigerate. Eat
cold from the fridge.

Black Sesame Crisps with Tuna

Makes approximately
24 biscuits, roughly 2cm
in diameter

35g plain flour
¼ teaspoon salt
4g golden caster sugar
20g unsalted butter
1 egg white
6ml dark soy sauce
black sesame seeds, for
**   sprinkling**
250g sashimi tuna, sliced
**   into 1.5cm pieces (from**
**   a fishmonger ideally)**
6 teaspoons wasabi paste,
**   to serve (optional)**

A fresh savoury snack to serve at afternoon tea or as a canapé at a party, these crisps would be just as delicious without the tuna, or with a topping of your choice.

Preheat the oven to 180°C/160°C (fan)/350°F/gas 4. Line two baking trays with parchment paper.

Sift the flour into a small bowl and add the salt and sugar.

Put the butter into a heatproof bowl and melt it in the microwave, then add the egg white and soy sauce. Pour this mixture into the flour and whisk until thoroughly combined.

Take ¼ teaspoon of the mixture and place it on the baking tray. Using the back of the spoon, swirl in a circular motion until you have a 2cm wide circle. Continue this process until all the mixture is used, leaving a 1.5cm gap between the circles. Sprinkle each one generously with black sesame seeds.

Bake on the middle or bottom shelf of the oven for 8–10 minutes. The edges of the crisps should be slightly curled under and a dark brown colour. Remove from the oven and cool on wire racks. Once completely cool, store in an airtight container until needed.

To serve, lay the crisps out on a flat serving plate and lay a small piece of tuna on each one and top with ¼ teaspoon wasabi paste, if using. Serve immediately.

Plum Wine

On one of our last nights in Osaka, Japan, we went out for dinner with Faye and Julia to a small restaurant where no one spoke a word of English and the whole menu was written in Japanese. Through a mixture of sign language and guesswork we ordered a delicious dinner, with Julia ordering an amazing drink none of us had heard of before – plum wine with soda water and ice. Since then, we have introduced the rest of the bakery to its delights and created two recipes with it.

Plum wine, or Umeshu in Japanese, is a sweet, alcoholic (about 15% proof) drink that is extremely popular in Japan, Korea and China, but quite hard to find in the UK. It is made from green (unripe) or yellow (ripe) ume fruit – a type of Japanese plum – which is soaked in a clear spirit called shochu with sugar. It is served either alone with plenty of ice, or with ice and soda water, and comes in beautifully decorated glass bottles.

For the afternoon tea, a glass or two of plum wine and soda water would be the perfect accompaniment to the cakes and macaroons, alongside some jasmine or other perfumed tea.

COCKTAILS & CUPCAKES

As well as our shared love of afternoon tea, we often find a cocktail can be a good antidote to a long day's baking and icing. We first realized that alcohol could work well in cupcakes when we worked with Sipsmith, an independent distiller based in West London, who subsequently provided us with some of their amazing bottles of gin and vodka to help develop our recipes.

Many of the ingredients in the cocktails can easily be translated into flavours for cupcakes, and from our first attempt at a gin and tonic version we are now working on many, many different types of 'alcoholic' cupcake. The bakery kitchen often resembles a bar and we are constantly thinking of new cocktail-cupcakes to try. Traditionally, people associate cupcakes with children, but the addition of alcohol has given the cupcake a new twist for adults, which is proving very popular. Many of these recipes would be even better served alongside their namesake drink.

BELLINI CUPCAKES

One of Italy's favourite drinks, the Bellini dates to some time around 1934 and was developed in Harry's Bar in Venice. The combination of peaches and champagne in this cupcake works extremely well, and we decorated ours with some sour peach sweets to give it extra kick.

Makes 12 regular cupcakes

1 x 400g tin peaches
95g unsalted butter, at room temperature
150g golden caster sugar
2 large eggs, free-range or organic
225g self-raising flour
½ teaspoon salt
220g peach purée (to make this, drain a tin of peaches and blend for 3 to 4 minutes in a food processor)
60ml peach juice/nectar
3 tablespoons peach jam
sour peach sweets, to decorate

Preheat the oven to 180°C/160°C (fan)/350°F/gas 4. Line a 12-hole muffin tray with muffin cases.

Drain the peaches, reserving the juice, and blend them in a food processor for 3–4 minutes until you have a purée. Set aside.

Cream the butter and sugar together using an electric hand beater until light and fluffy. Add the eggs to the mixture one at a time, ensuring each one is well incorporated before adding the next.

Add the flour and salt to the mixture and beat on a low speed until just combined. Pour in the peach purée and reserved juice and mix again on a low speed until everything is well mixed.

Divide the batter equally between the muffin cases and bake in the oven for 20–23 minutes, or until an inserted skewer comes out clean. Brush each cupcake with a thin layer of peach jam and leave to cool on a wire rack.

CHAMPAGNE BUTTERCREAM ICING

80g unsalted butter, at room temperature
45ml champagne
330g icing sugar

FOR THE CHAMPAGNE REDUCTION
250ml champagne

To make the champagne reduction, pour the champagne into a small pan set over a medium to high heat on the hob. Bring to the boil, then reduce the heat and let it simmer for approximately 10 minutes, or until the champagne is reduced to approximately 2 tablespoons of liquid. Keep an eye on the liquid, as it can dry up and burn very quickly. Once it is done, set aside to cool.

Put the butter, champagne reduction, champagne and half the icing sugar into a bowl. Beat with an electric hand beater on a low speed until all the ingredients are well mixed. Add the remaining icing sugar and beat on a low speed until everything is combined. Increase the speed to medium/high and beat for a further minute, until light and fluffy.

Ice each cupcake with champagne buttercream icing and top with a sour peach sweet.

GIN AND TONIC CUPCAKES

Makes 12 regular cupcakes

FOR THE GIN AND TONIC SYRUP
85ml tonic water
juice of 1½ lemons
100g granulated sugar
1 lemon, finely sliced
85ml gin

FOR THE SPONGE
150g golden caster sugar
140g self-raising flour
17g cornflour
⅔ teaspoon baking powder
150g unsalted butter, at room temperature
3 large eggs, preferably free-range or organic
½ teaspoon good-quality vanilla extract
2 tablespoons milk
zest of 1½ lemons

This was the first cupcake we created with alcohol in both the sponge and icing, and we now sell them on a regular basis in our shops. We try to ensure that children are not eating them, but some have been known to, and they seem to go down very well!

Preheat the oven to 180°C/160°C (fan)/350°F/gas 4. Line a 12-hole muffin tray with muffin cases.

First make the syrup by combining the tonic water, lemon juice and sugar in a pan. Place on the hob and bring to the boil, then turn down the heat and simmer for 3–5 minutes, until it becomes syrup-like. Add the lemon slices and simmer for another 2 minutes. Remove from the heat, add the gin and stir again. Allow to cool, then strain. Reserve 60ml of the syrup to use in the icing, and set the rest aside until needed.

In a food processor, mix the sugar, flour, cornflour and baking powder until well combined. Add the rest of the ingredients and process very briefly (roughly 10 seconds) until evenly mixed.

Divide the batter evenly between the muffin cases and bake in the oven for about 15–18 minutes, until risen and golden brown and an inserted skewer comes out clean.

Take the cupcakes out of the oven and brush the surface of each one with some of the gin and tonic syrup. Then brush them again with more syrup. Allow to cool in the tray for about 10 minutes, then transfer them to a wire rack to cool fully before icing, by which time the syrup will have soaked through the sponge.

GIN AND TONIC ICING

115g unsalted butter, at room temperature
60ml reserved gin and tonic syrup (see above)
1 teaspoon good-quality vanilla extract
500g icing sugar, sifted
candied lemon slices or lemon zest, to decorate

Beat the butter, syrup, vanilla extract and half the icing sugar in a bowl until smooth. This will usually take a few minutes. Gradually add the remainder of the icing sugar to produce a buttercream of a creamy and smooth consistency.

Ice each cupcake with the icing, and decorate with a candied lemon slice, some lemon zest or a slice of lemon.

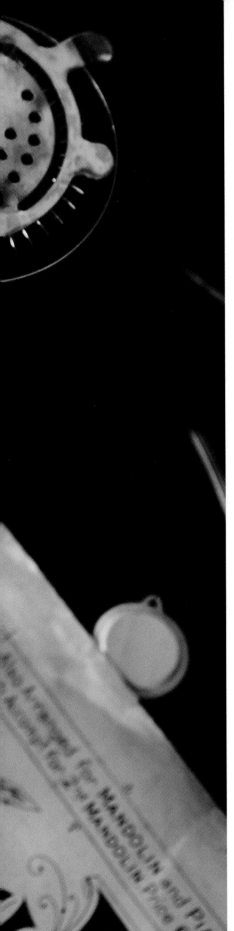

WHITE CARGO CUPCAKES

Makes 12 regular cupcakes

FOR THE VANILLA AND GIN SYRUP
160g granulated sugar
160ml water
1 vanilla pod
(reserve the seeds)
160ml gin

FOR THE SPONGE
210g self-raising flour
25g cornflour
225g golden caster sugar
1 teaspoon baking powder
1 teaspoon ground nutmeg
¼ teaspoon ground cinnamon
4 large eggs, preferably
free-range or organic
225g unsalted butter, at
room temperature
½ teaspoon good-quality
vanilla extract
3 tablespoons milk

White Cargo is a fairly obscure cocktail that is made with vanilla ice cream and dates from the Venezuela of the 1920s. In fact, the flavours might work better as a cupcake than in a cocktail.

Preheat the oven to 180°C/160°C (fan)/350°F/gas 4. Line a 12-hole muffin tray with muffin cases.

First make the vanilla and gin syrup. Put the sugar, water and vanilla pod into a pan. Place on the hob over a medium heat until the sugar is completely dissolved. Then turn the heat up and bring to the boil. Boil for about 8–10 minutes. Remove from the heat, add the gin and stir to combine.

Now make the sponge. Put all the dry ingredients into a food processor and mix for 10 seconds. Add the eggs, butter, vanilla extract and milk and blitz for about 30 seconds, stopping halfway through to scrape down any batter that has got stuck around the sides of the processor.

Spoon the batter into the muffin cases, filling each about two-thirds full. Bake in the centre of the oven for approximately 20–25 minutes, until slightly raised and golden brown and an inserted skewer comes out clean.

Remove the cupcakes from the oven and leave them to cool in the tray for about 10 minutes, then prick the surface of each one with a fork and brush 6–8 times with the syrup to really soak the sponge. Allow to cool fully on a wire rack before icing.

GIN AND VANILLA BUTTERCREAM ICING

115g unsalted butter, at
room temperature
60ml gin
500g icing sugar
1 teaspoon good-quality
vanilla extract
scraped seeds from the
vanilla pod
ground nutmeg, to decorate
(optional)

Place the butter, gin and half the icing sugar in a bowl. Beat with an electric hand beater on a low speed until all the ingredients are combined. Add the remaining icing sugar, vanilla extract and seeds and beat again until thoroughly mixed.

These cupcakes look lovely undecorated, as the vanilla seeds are visible in the icing and give a lovely finish. Or you could try a light sprinkling of ground nutmeg.

AVIATION CUPCAKES

Makes 12 regular cupcakes

**FOR THE LEMON AND
GIN SYRUP**
160g granulated sugar
160ml water
1 lemon, thinly sliced
160ml gin

FOR THE SPONGE
230g self-raising flour
25g cornflour
230g golden caster sugar
1½ teaspoons baking powder
**4 large eggs, preferably
free-range or organic**
**230g unsalted butter, at
room temperature**
juice and zest of 2 lemons
**12 maraschino cherries,
to decorate**

The first Aviation cocktails were made in the early twentieth century in the USA, their name inspired by the pale sky-blue colour of the crème de violette. Sipsmith gave us the idea of making an Aviation cupcake. The cocktails are not as widely available these days, but Sipsmith made them for their cocktail and cupcake evening and we hope they will soon enjoy a revival. We have added a bit of blue food colouring to our icing to give it a sky-blue tint in keeping with its history.

Preheat the oven to 180°C/160°C (fan)/350°F/gas 4. Line a 12-hole muffin tray with muffin cases.

First make the lemon and gin syrup. Put the sugar and water into a saucepan and place on the hob over a medium heat until the sugar is dissolved. Turn the heat up and bring to the boil. Boil for about 8 minutes, then add the lemon slices and boil for a further minute. Remove from the heat, add the gin and stir to combine.

Now make the sponge. Put the flour, cornflour, sugar and baking powder into a food processor and mix for 10 seconds. Add the eggs, butter, lemon juice and zest and blitz for about 30 seconds, stopping halfway through to scrape down any batter that has got stuck around the sides of the processor.

Spoon the batter into the muffin cases, filling each about two-thirds full. Put a maraschino cherry on the top of each one, just resting in the batter. Bake in the centre of the oven for approximately 20–25 minutes, until slightly raised and golden brown and an inserted skewer comes out clean.

Remove the cupcakes from the oven. Leave them to cool in the tray for about 10 minutes, then prick the surface of each one with a fork and brush 6–8 times with the syrup to really soak the sponge. Allow to cool fully on a wire rack before icing with the violet liqueur buttercream (see page 144).

VIOLET LIQUEUR BUTTERCREAM ICING

115g unsalted butter, at room temperature
60ml violet liqueur/crème de violette
500g icing sugar
a few drops of blue food colouring
crystallized violets or fresh blueberries,
**   to decorate (optional)**

Place the butter, violet liqueur and half the icing sugar in a bowl. Beat with an electric hand beater on a low speed until all the ingredients are combined. Add the remaining icing sugar and beat again until thoroughly mixed. Add one or two drops of food colouring and beat to give you a smooth, pale blue icing.

Once the cupcakes are iced, decorate with some crystallized violets or fresh blueberries if desired.

MOSCOW MULE
CUPCAKES

Makes 12 regular cupcakes

FOR THE GINGER AND
VODKA SYRUP
30g fresh ginger
160g granulated sugar
160ml water
160ml vodka

FOR THE SPONGE
210g self-raising flour
225g golden caster sugar
25g cornflour
1 teaspoon baking powder
1 tablespoon ground ginger
**4 large eggs, preferably
    free-range or organic**
**225g unsalted butter, at
    room temperature**
3 tablespoons milk
**4 pieces of stem ginger,
chopped**

*A delicious mix of vodka, ginger beer and lime, the Moscow Mule
originated in the US in the 1940s and was thought to be behind the
rise in popularity in vodka in the States in the 1950s. The 'Moscow'
in the name is believed to come from the fact that vodka was
always thought to be Russian. This cocktail is probably one of our
favourites, and as ginger and lime were already popular flavours
at the bakery, this cupcake was always going to be a winner.*

Preheat the oven to 180°C/160°C (fan)/350°F/gas 4. Line a 12-hole
muffin tray with muffin cases.

First make the ginger and vodka syrup. Peel and thinly slice the
ginger. Put it into a pan with the sugar and water and bring to
the boil, allowing the sugar to dissolve completely. Boil for about
5 minutes, then remove from the heat. Add the vodka and stir
to combine.

Now make the sponge. Put the flour, sugar, cornflour, baking
powder and ground ginger into a food processor and mix for
10 seconds. Add the eggs, butter and milk and blitz for about
30 seconds, stopping halfway through to scrape down any batter
that has got stuck around the sides of the processor. Transfer to
a medium-sized bowl and fold in the chopped ginger.

Spoon the batter into the muffin cases, filling each about
two-thirds full. Bake in the centre of the oven for approximately
20–25 minutes, until slightly raised and golden brown and an
inserted skewer comes out clean.

Remove the cupcakes from the oven and leave to cool in the tray
for about 10 minutes, then prick the surface of each one with a fork
and brush 5–6 times with the syrup below. Allow to cool fully on
a wire rack before icing with the lime and vodka buttercream (see
page 148).

LIME AND VODKA BUTTERCREAM ICING

115g unsalted butter
45ml vodka
500g icing sugar
2 tablespoons lime juice
zest of 1 lime
12 pieces of crystallized ginger, to decorate

Place the butter, vodka and half the icing sugar in a bowl. Beat with an electric hand beater until all the ingredients are combined. Add the remaining icing sugar and the lime juice and zest and beat again until thoroughly combined.

Once the cupcakes are iced, decorate each one with a piece of crystallized ginger. If you prefer, you can make your own by slicing some pieces of stem ginger in half and rolling them in granulated sugar.

SIPSMITH™
independent spirits

SIPSMITH™
independent spirits
MONTECRISTI
DISTILLED CIGAR!

SIPSMITH™
independent spirits

Barley
VODKA

Barley
VODKA

LEMON
VODKA
13/12/10

35cl e   COPPER STILLED IN LONDON   40% vol

35cl e   COPPER STILLED IN LONDON   40% vol

Makes 12 regular cupcakes

2 pears
50ml vodka
110g unsalted butter, at
    room temperature
225g caster sugar
2 large eggs
120ml pear juice
2 teaspoons vodka from the
    soaked pears (see below)
150g self-raising flour
125g plain flour

FOR THE PEAR VODKA ICING
100g softened butter
450g icing sugar
vodka from the soaked pears,
    to taste
chocolate olives, to decorate
    (optional)

This cupcake version of a fruit-flavoured vodka martini is perfectly complemented by a chocolate olive. (We've used Rococo's).

Peel the pears and cut them into 12 large cubes. Place in a small container, cover with the vodka and leave to soak. The strength of the flavour depends how long you leave them, but we would recommend at least 2 hours or overnight in the fridge for a more intense flavour.

When you are ready to bake the cupcakes, preheat the oven to 180°C/160°C (fan)/350°F/gas 4 and line a 12-hole muffin tray with muffin cases.

Cream the butter and sugar in a bowl until the mixture is pale and smooth. Add the eggs, one at a time, mixing briefly after each addition. This can take a few minutes. Scrape down the sides of the bowl with a rubber spatula to ensure the mixture stays well combined.

Put the pear juice and vodka into a plastic measuring jug.

Combine the two flours in a separate bowl. Add one-third of the flour to the combined butter and sugar mixture and beat well. Pour in one-third of the pear juice and vodka and beat again. Repeat these steps until all the flour and juice and vodka has been added. Carefully and evenly spoon the mixture into the muffin cases. Place one piece of vodka-soaked pear in each cupcake.

Bake in the centre of the oven for approximately 25 minutes, until slightly raised and golden brown and an inserted skewer comes out clean. Remove from the oven, leave in the tray for 10 minutes or so, then place carefully on a wire rack to cool.

In a bowl, beat the butter and icing sugar together, then add the vodka and beat again to create a smooth buttercream icing. Top each cooled cupcake with icing and decorate.

MOJITO CUPCAKES

A very popular, refreshing cocktail that dates back to Cuba in the nineteenth century, when it was made with aquardiente, an early version of rum. The mint, lime and sugar work well to counter the strong taste of the rum.

Makes 12 regular cupcakes (on top tier opposite)

FOR THE RUM AND LIME SYRUP
160g granulated sugar
160ml water
1 lime, sliced
160ml white rum

FOR THE SPONGE
230g self-raising flour
230g golden caster sugar
25g cornflour
1½ teaspoons baking powder
230g unsalted butter, at room temperature
4 large eggs, preferably free-range or organic
juice and zest of 2 limes

Preheat the oven to 180°C/160°C (fan)/350°F/gas 4. Line a 12-hole muffin tray with muffin cases.

First make the rum and lime syrup. Put the sugar and water into a pan and bring to a boil on the hob, allowing the sugar to dissolve completely. Boil for about 8 minutes, then add the sliced lime and continue boiling for a further minute. Remove from the heat and stir in the rum.

Now make the sponge. Put the flour, sugar, cornflour and baking powder into a food processor and mix for 10 seconds. Add the remaining ingredients and process again for about 30 seconds, stopping halfway through to scrape down any batter that has got stuck around the sides of the processor.

Spoon the batter into the muffin cases, filling each about two-thirds full. Bake in the centre of the oven for approximately 20–25 minutes, until slightly raised and golden brown and an inserted skewer comes out clean.

Remove the cupcakes from the oven. Leave to cool in the tray for about 10 minutes, then prick the surface of each one with a fork and brush 5 or 6 times with the syrup. Allow to cool fully on a wire rack before icing.

LIME AND RUM BUTTERCREAM ICING

115g unsalted butter
45ml white rum
500g icing sugar
2 tablespoons lime juice
zest of 1 lime

FOR THE CRYSTALLIZED MINT LEAF DECORATION
12 mint leaves (or more, depending on size)
1 egg white
100g granulated sugar

To make the decoration, dip or brush the mint leaves with egg white. Cover with granulated sugar and leave to dry on a piece of kitchen towel for a couple of hours. Do not leave them any longer or they will turn black.

To make the buttercream icing, place the butter, rum and half the icing sugar in a bowl. Beat with an electric hand beater on a low speed until all the ingredients are combined. Add the remaining icing sugar, the lime juice and zest and beat again until thoroughly combined.

Ice the cupcakes with the buttercream and decorate each one with 1 or 2 of the mint leaves, depending on how many you have made.

STRAWBERRY DAIQUIRI CUPCAKES

The favourite drink of Ernest Hemingway and John F Kennedy, the Daiquiri was originally from Cuba. The strawberries are a more recent addition and work exceptionally well in this cupcake version. The purée is also delicious eaten alone!

Makes 12 cupcakes (on middle tier on page 153)

FOR THE STRAWBERRY AND RUM PURÉE
500g strawberries, hulled
50g granulated sugar
1 teaspoon cornflour
50ml white rum

FOR THE LIME SPONGE
230g unsalted butter
230g golden caster sugar
4 large eggs, preferably free-range or organic
25g cornflour
230g self-raising flour
1½ teaspoon baking powder
2 limes, juiced and zested

Preheat the oven to 180°C/160°C (fan)/350°F/gas 4. Line a 12 hole muffin tray with muffin cases.

To make the purée, blend the strawberries, sugar and cornflour for a minute until smooth. Transfer to a pan and cook over a medium heat for 20 minutes, stirring occasionally. Remove from the heat, stir in the rum and leave to cool completely.

To make the sponge, cream the butter and sugar together in a bowl until light and fluffy. Add the eggs, one at a time, ensuring each one is mixed well after each addition. Combine the flours and baking powder in a seperate bowl and beat this into the egg, butter and sugar mixture in thirds, alternating with the lime juice and zest.

Spoon the batter into the cases, filling each about two-thirds full. Bake in the centre of the oven for 20–25 minutes until slightly raised and golden brown and an inserted cake skewer comes out clean. Remove from the oven, leave to cool in the tray for 10 minutes then turn out on to a wire rack to cool completely.

Once cool, cut a teaspoon-sized piece from the top of each cupcake and fill with puree. Try not to let any spill out.

RUM ICING

115g unsalted butter
60ml white rum
500g icing sugar
1tbsp lime juice
zest of 1 lime
12 fresh strawberries, hulled, to decorate

Place the butter, rum and half the icing sugar into a bowl. Beat on a low speed until all the ingredients are combined. Add the remaining icing sugar and beat again on a low speed until thoroughly combined. Add the lime juice and zest and beat on a high speed for one further minute.

Once the cupcakes are iced, decorate with a fresh strawberry in the centre of each cake.

MARGARITA CUPCAKES

It is thought that the Margarita dates back to 1940s Mexico, although it has since become one of the most popular cocktails the world over. There are now many different flavours of Margarita available, but for our cupcakes we have kept to the classic ingredients of tequila, lime and salt.

Makes 12 cupcakes (on bottom tier on page 153)

FOR THE TEQUILA AND LIME SYRUP
160g granulated sugar
160ml water
1 lime, sliced
160ml tequila

FOR THE SPONGE
230g unsalted butter, at room temperature
230g golden caster sugar
4 large eggs, preferably free-range or organic
230g self-raising flour
25g cornflour
1½ teaspoons baking powder
juice and zest of 2 limes

Preheat the oven to 180°C/160°C (fan)/350°F/gas 4. Line a 12-hole muffin tray with muffin cases.

To make the syrup, bring the sugar and water to the boil in a small pan on the hob. Simmer on a medium-to-high heat for 8 minutes. Add the sliced lime and cook for a further 1 to 2 minutes. Set aside to cool for 20–25 minutes until cooled but still warm to touch. Stir in the tequila.

Now make the sponge. Cream the butter and sugar together in a bowl until light and fluffy. Add the eggs one at a time, ensuring each one is mixed in well before adding the next. Combine the flours and baking powder in a seperate bowl and beat into the egg, butter and sugar mixture in thirds, alternating with the lime juice and zest.

Spoon the batter into the cases, filling each about two-thirds full. Bake in the centre of the oven for 20–25 minutes, until slightly raised and golden brown and an inserted skewer comes out clean.

Remove the cupcakes from the oven. Leave to cool slightly, then prick the surface of each one with a fork and brush 4 times with the syrup. Ensure all the syrup has been absorbed before applying the next coat. Transfer to a wire rack to cool completely.

LIME AND TEQUILA BUTTERCREAM ICING

115g unsalted butter, at room temperature
60ml tequila
500g icing sugar
1 tablespoon lime juice
zest of 1 lime
lime salt, for decoration (a handful of sea salt or fleur de sel, mixed with lime zest)

Place the butter, tequila and half the icing sugar in a bowl. Beat with an electric hand beater on a low speed until combined. Add the remaining icing sugar and beat again on a low speed until thoroughly mixed. Add the lime juice and zest and beat on a high speed for 1 further minute.

Once the cupcakes are iced, sprinkle a little lime salt over the top of them to decorate.

TEQUILA SUNRISE CUPCAKES

Our Tequila Sunrise Cupcakes look more like sunset cupcakes, with their red/orange surfaces giving way to yellow sponge underneath. We have based this cupcake on the more recent version of the Tequila Sunrise cocktail, developed in California in the 1970s.

Makes 12 regular cupcakes

FOR THE TEQUILA AND GRENADINE SYRUP
80ml grenadine
80ml tequila

FOR THE SPONGE
230g unsalted butter, at room temperature
230g golden caster sugar
4 large eggs, preferably free-range or organic
230g self-raising flour
25g cornflour
1½ teaspoons baking powder
juice and zest of 1 orange

Preheat the oven to 180°C/160°C (fan)/350°F/gas 4. Line a 12-hole muffin tray with muffin cases.

Cream the butter and sugar together in a bowl until light and fluffy. Add the eggs one at a time, ensuring each one is well mixed in before you add the next one.

In a seperate bowl combine the flours and baking powder and beat into the egg, butter and sugar mixture in thirds, alternating with the orange juice and zest.

Spoon the batter into the muffin cases, filling each about two-thirds full. Bake in the centre of the oven for approximately 20–25 minutes, until slightly raised and golden brown and an inserted skewer comes out clean.

Remove from the oven and allow to cool in the tray for about 10 minutes. While they are cooling, make the syrup by simply mixing together the grenadine and tequila. Prick the surface of each cupcake with a fork and brush 5 or 6 times with the syrup to really soak the sponge. Allow to cool fully on a wire rack before icing.

ORANGE AND TEQUILA BUTTERCREAM ICING

115g unsalted butter, at room temperature
1–2 tablespoons tequila
500g icing sugar
juice of ½ orange
zest of 1 lime
12 glacé cherries and orange zest, to decorate

Place the butter, tequila and half the icing sugar in a bowl. Beat with an electric hand beater on a low speed until all the ingredients are combined. Add the remaining icing sugar and beat again on a low speed until thoroughly mixed. Add the orange juice and lime zest and beat on a high speed for a further minute.

Once the cupcakes are iced, decorate each one with a glacé cherry and some orange zest.

SUMMERCUP CUPCAKES

Makes 12–14 cupcakes

FOR THE SUMMERCUP SYRUP
75g granulated sugar
75ml water
zest of ½ a lemon
40ml Summercup (or Pimms)

FOR THE CUCUMBER MINT SPONGE
200g unsalted butter
225g golden caster sugar
3 large eggs, preferably free-range or organic
1 teaspoon good-quality vanilla extract
270g self-raising flour
½ teaspoon salt
170g grated cucumber
6g finely chopped fresh mint leaves

Using Sipsmith's amazing Summercup – a mixture of their dry gin blended with Earl Grey tea, lemon verbena and cucumber – as inspiration, this cupcake has a unique, fresh taste that is perfect on a summer's day.

Preheat the oven to 180°C/160°C (fan)/350°F/gas 4. Line a 12-hole muffin tray with muffin cases. (You may want to line an extra 6-hole muffin tray to use up any excess batter.)

First make the syrup. Place the sugar, water and lemon zest in a small pan and bring to the boil on the hob. Allow to simmer on a medium to high heat for 2–3 minutes. Remove from the heat and set aside to cool for 20–25 minutes. Once the liquid has cooled and is warm to touch, pour in the Summercup liqueur and stir to combine.

Now make the sponge. Cream the butter and sugar together in a bowl until light and fluffy. Add the eggs, one at a time, ensuring each one is mixed well after each addition. Add the vanilla extract and beat again. Add the flour and salt and mix until just combined. Finally, fold the cucumber and mint into the batter and fold in with a spatula until well combined.

Spoon the batter into the cases, filling each about two-thirds full. Bake in the centre of the oven for approx. 20–25 minutes until slightly raised and golden brown or a cake skewer inserted in the centre of the cakes comes out clean. Remove from the oven. Allow to cool slightly, then prick the surface with a fork and, using a pastry brush, brush the syrup onto each cake 4 times. Ensure all the syrup is absorbed before applying the next coat then cool fully on a wire rack.

SUMMERCUP BUTTERCREAM ICING

135g unsalted butter
30ml Summercup (or Pimms)
340g icing sugar
sliced cucumber, to decorate (optional)

Place the butter, Summercup liqueur and half the icing sugar in a bowl. Beat with an electric hand beater on a low speed until all the ingredients are combined. Add the remaining icing sugar and beat again on a low speed until thoroughly combined. Beat on a high speed for one further minute. Ice the cupcakes and decorate with the cucumber, if you like.

NEGRONI CUPCAKES

Makes approximately
15 regular cupcakes

FOR THE SPONGE

**200g unsalted butter, at
room temperature**
230g golden caster sugar
zest of 1 orange
**3 eggs, preferably free-range
or organic**
250g self-raising flour
½ teaspoon salt
80ml milk
30ml Campari
30ml vermouth rosso

FOR THE NEGRONI SYRUP

50g granulated sugar
50ml water
40ml gin
40ml vermouth rosso

*A popular Italian pre-dinner drink that is more bitter than sweet
and a beautiful orange/red colour, the Negroni dates back to
Florence 1919, where it was adapted from another popular Italian
cocktail, the Americano. These cupcakes have a distinctive flavour,
and are decorated with candied oranges which really make them
stand out.*

Preheat the oven to 180°C/160°C (fan)/350°F/gas 4. Line a 12-hole
muffin tray and a 6-hole one with muffin cases.

Put the butter, sugar and orange zest into a bowl and cream
with an electric hand beater until light and fluffy.

Add the eggs one at a time, beating well after each addition.
Sift the flour and salt on top of the batter and beat on a low speed
until it has all been incorporated.

Pour in the milk, Campari and vermouth and beat until the
mixture is smooth.

Divide evenly between the muffin cases and bake in the oven
for 18–20 minutes, or until golden brown and an inserted skewer
comes out clean. Remove from the oven and leave to cool in the
tray for about 10 minutes then transfer to a wire rack to cool
completely.

While the cupcakes are cooling, make the syrup. Place the sugar
and water into a small pan and bring to the boil on the hob.
Simmer on a medium to high heat for 2–3 minutes, then remove
from the heat and set aside to cool for 20–25 minutes. Once
the liquid has cooled and is warm to touch, pour in the gin and
vermouth and stir to combine. Brush the syrup onto each cupcake
4 times, ensuring all the syrup is absorbed before applying the
next coat, then top with Negroni Buttercream Icing and a slice of
Candied Orange (see page 163).

NEGRONI
BUTTERCREAM ICING

130g unsalted butter, at room temperature
zest of ½ orange
25ml Campari
20ml vermouth rosso
30ml gin
450g icing sugar

Place the butter, orange zest, Campari, vermouth, gin and half the icing sugar into a bowl. Beat on a low speed, using an electric hand beater, until all the ingredients are combined.

Add the remaining icing sugar and beat again on a low speed until thoroughly combined. Beat on high speed for a further minute.

Ice each cupcake with some of the icing and decorate each one with a candied orange slice (see below).

CANDIED ORANGES

300ml water, plus extra for topping up
100g granulated sugar
3 oranges, cut horizontally into 0.5cm slices

Put the water and sugar into a frying pan and bring to the boil on the hob. Place the oranges into the syrup in a single layer. Do not overlap them. Turn down the heat so that the syrup is simmering gently. Simmer for about 30–35 minutes, turning the oranges every 10 minutes. They will be ready when the peel becomes translucent. Remove and drain on kitchen paper. Repeat until all the slices have been candied, adding more water as necessary.

OLD FASHIONED CUPCAKE

Makes 12 regular cupcakes

160g unsalted butter,
   at room temperature
250g golden caster sugar
zest of 1 orange
2 large eggs, free-range
   or organic
250g self-raising flour
a pinch of salt
100ml bourbon whiskey

FOR THE OLD-FASHIONED
ICING
150g unsalted butter
375g icing sugar
15 dashes of angostura bitters
45ml bourbon whiskey
12 x maraschino or glacé
   cherries on wooden
   cocktail sticks, to decorate

Don Draper's favourite drink in the TV series Mad Men, *the 'Old Fashioned' contains bourbon whiskey and dates back to 1880s Kentucky. This cupcake was suggested by Martha's brother Daniel, who has been living in New York where it has become extremely popular in recent years.*

Preheat the oven to 180°C/160°C (fan)/350°F/gas 4. Line a 12-hole muffin tray with muffin cases.

Cream the butter and sugar together in a bowl until light and fluffy. Add the orange zest and the eggs and beat with an electric hand beater until well combined and the batter is smooth and fluffy. Add the flour and salt and mix on a low speed until just combined.

Pour in the whiskey and beat until everything is well combined and you have a smooth batter.

Divide the mixture evenly between the muffin cases and bake in the oven for 15–20 minutes, until golden brown and an inserted skewer comes out clean.

Remove from the oven. Allow the cupcakes to cool in the tray for 10 minutes, then turn out onto a wire rack to cool fully.

Combine the ingredients for the icing in a bowl and beat on a low speed until combined. Increase the speed of the beater to medium/high and beat for a further minute, until the icing is light and fluffy.

Ice each cupcake and decorate with a cherry on a cocktail stick, stuck into the icing at an angle.

Christmas and New Year

Christmas and New Year always mean lots of opportunities to get together with family and friends, and there is usually plenty of food, if not too much. Edible gifts make lovely presents, and any of the following recipes would work well as gifts in a box tied with ribbon.

We sell a great many of these cakes throughout the year but they work particularly well at Christmas, as they are slightly more indulgent than some of our other recipes.

The lead up to Christmas is always an exciting time at the bakery – there is a fantastic, festive atmosphere in the shops and everyone fights over the Christmas Eve shift, which is probably one of the nicest days of the year to work, and not only because it is a half-day rather than a full one!

Chocolate and Marshmallow Layer Cake

Makes two 20cm cakes, which can be sandwiched together to make one layer cake

230g good-quality dark chocolate (70% cocoa if possible)
170g unsalted butter, at room temperature
350g soft brown sugar
3 large eggs, separated
370g plain flour
1½ teaspoons baking powder
1½ teaspoons bicarbonate of soda
½ teaspoon salt
500ml semi-skimmed milk, at room temperature
2 teaspoons vanilla extract

This variation on our popular chocolate cake makes the ideal Christmas cake for the centre of the table. Its snow-like icing can be decorated with all sorts of plastic or sugar Christmas decorations to create the perfect Christmas scene.

Preheat the oven to 190°C/170°C (fan)/375°F/gas 5. Grease and line the bases of two 20cm cake tins, slightly deeper than regular sandwich tins.

Break the chocolate into small pieces and melt, either in the microwave on a medium heat at 10–20 second intervals and stirring well in between, or in a heatproof bowl over a pan of simmering water on the hob, making sure the bowl doesn't touch the water. Be careful not to burn the chocolate. Leave to cool slightly.

Cream the butter and sugar together, using an electric hand beater, until pale and smooth. In a separate bowl and with clean beaters, beat the egg yolks for several minutes. Slowly add the egg yolks to the creamed butter and sugar mixture and beat well. Next, add the melted chocolate and beat well again.

Combine the flour, baking powder, bicarbonate of soda and salt in a seperate bowl. Put the milk and vanilla into a jug. Add one third of the flour mixture to the chocolate, butter and sugar, alternating with one third of the milk and vanilla mixture and beating very well after each addition. Repeat until all the flour and milk mixtures have been added.

In a clean bowl, whisk the egg whites until soft peaks start to form. Carefully fold the egg whites into the main batter using a metal spoon. Do not beat or you will take all the air out of the cake.

Divide the mixture evenly into the tins and bake in the oven for about 30 minutes, until an inserted skewer comes out clean. Remove from the oven and leave the cakes in the tins for about 10 minutes before turning out onto wire racks to cool. Remove the lining paper from the base. Finish with the chocolate buttercream and the marshmallow icing (see pages 172-73).

Chocolate Buttercream Icing

175g dark chocolate (at least 70% cocoa solids)
115g unsalted butter, at room temperature
½ tablespoon semi-skimmed milk
½ teaspoon good-quality vanilla extract
125g icing sugar, sifted

Break the chocolate into small pieces and melt, either in the microwave on a medium heat at 10–20 second intervals and stirring well in between, or in a bowl over a pan of simmering water on the hob, making sure the bowl doesn't touch the water. Be careful not to burn the chocolate. Leave to cool slightly.

Beat the butter, sugar, milk and vanilla in a bowl, using an electric hand beater, until smooth. Add the melted chocolate and beat until thick and creamy.

Marshmallow Icing

180g granulated sugar
120g golden syrup
2¼ tablespoons water
3 large egg whites
½ teaspoon good-quality vanilla extract (optional)
Christmas-themed decorations and edible glitter,
   to decorate (optional)

Place the sugar, golden syrup and water in a pan or shallow frying pan and place over a high heat on the hob until the mixture reaches the 'soft ball' stage – this is when the bubbles in the mixture almost start to stick together and would drop off a spoon in a smooth, slow stream. This could take about 2 minutes. When it reaches this stage, remove from the heat.

Whisk the egg whites in a mixing bowl until soft peaks start to form. Using an electric mixer or Magimix on a low speed, slowly and evenly pour the hot sugar mixture into the egg whites. Continue to beat on a low speed until all the hot sugar is in the mixing bowl.

Turn the mixer up to medium-high speed and continue beating the mixture until it becomes thick, glossy and cool. If you like add ½ teaspoon of vanilla extract towards the end of the mixing process.

As this icing is easiest to work with while it is still a bit warm, try to use it right away. If you do have some left over, you can store it in the fridge overnight, but not for longer.

To assemble the cake, place a layer of the sponge on a plate and cover with the chocolate buttercream icing. Place the other layer of cake on top and cover the top and sides of the cake with the marshmallow icing, swirling it on the top to make snow-like peaks. Decorate with some Christmas themed decorations and perhaps some edible glitter.

Christmas Trifle Cupcakes

This recipe was created to sell in one of the supermarkets for the publication of our second book. It also proved very popular in our shops at Christmas time, as a cake alternative to a traditional trifle.

Makes 14–15 regular cupcakes

FOR THE SPONGE
225g caster sugar
1 teaspoon baking powder
280g self-raising flour
25g cornflour
240g tinned peaches, drained and puréed
225g unsalted butter, at room temperature
4 large eggs, preferably free-range or organic
¼ teaspoon almond extract
15 teaspoons good-quality raspberry jam

Preheat the oven to 180°C/160°C (fan)/350°F/gas 4. Line two 12-hole muffin trays with muffin cases.

Put the sugar, baking powder, flour, cornflour and peaches into a food processor. Pulse until evenly mixed (roughly 4 seconds). Add the rest of the ingredients and process briefly until combined (roughly 10 seconds). If you prefer to use an electric hand beater, cream the butter and sugar together first, beat in the eggs one by one, then add the remaining ingredients and beat well together.

Divide the mixture evenly into the muffin cases. Bake for 25 minutes or until cooked. The cakes will appear fairly moist, even when cooked. Remove from the oven and allow to cool in the tray for 10 minutes before placing on a wire rack to cool completely.

Carefully make a small hole in the centre of each cupcake and place a small amount (roughly a teaspoon) of raspberry jam into the sponge. Discard (or eat!) the small amount of sponge you have removed.

Custard Buttercream Icing

115g unsalted butter, at room temperature
90ml semi-skimmed milk
150g custard powder
400g icing sugar, sifted
a few drops yellow food colouring
flaked almonds, to decorate (either used straight from the packet or lightly toasted on a baking tray for a few minutes in the oven)

Beat the butter, milk, custard powder and half the icing sugar until smooth. This will usually take a few minutes. Gradually add the rest of the icing sugar to produce a buttercream of a creamy and smooth consistency. Carefully add a few drops of yellow food colouring and beat well to get your desired colour.

The buttercream can be stored in an airtight container for up to 3 days at room temperature. Before re-using, beat well. If it has hardened, simply add some milk, a little at a time, and beat until the desired consistency is reached

Ice each cupcake with a spoonful of the buttercream icing and sprinkle a handful of flaked almonds over the top.

Mulled Wine Cupcakes

The most Christmas-flavoured cupcake we could think of, this rich, spicy sponge is offset perfectly by the light icing. It would make a great Christmas gift for friends or could be left out for Father Christmas and his reindeer on Christmas Eve, with a glass of sherry alongside.

Makes 12 regular cupcakes

FOR THE MULLED WINE
175ml red wine
1 cinnamon stick
4 cloves
zest of ½ orange

FOR THE SPONGE
90g butter, at room temperature
200g soft dark brown sugar
50g granulated sugar
1 egg, plus 1 egg yolk
1 medium glass (175ml) of mulled wine
1 teaspoon orange essence
¼ teaspoon bicarbonate of soda
½ teaspoon baking powder
¼ teaspoon salt
½ teaspoon ground cinnamon
50g good-quality cocoa powder
140g plain flour

Preheat the oven to 180°C/160°C (fan)/350°F/gas 4. Line a 12-hole muffin tray with muffin cases.

Heat the wine in a pan with the spices until it just comes to the boil, then remove from the heat, cover and leave to infuse for at least 30 minutes. Strain before using.

In a large bowl, cream together the butter and sugars until pale and fluffy. Add the egg and egg yolk, mix well, then add the mulled wine and orange essence and mix until the batter is evenly combined. Fold in all the dry ingredients with a metal spoon until just combined.

Divide the mixture evenly between the muffin cases and bake in the oven for approximately 20 minutes, until an inserted skewer comes out clean. Remove the cupcakes from the oven and leave to cool in the tray for 10 minutes or so before turning out onto a wire rack to cool completely.

Spiced Mascarpone Icing

50g unsalted butter, at room temperature
juice and zest of ½ orange
¼ teaspoon ground cinnamon
175g icing sugar
125g mascarpone

Put the butter, orange juice and zest, cinnamon and half the icing sugar in a bowl and beat, using an electric hand beater on a low speed, until smooth. Add the rest of the icing sugar and beat again until well combined.

Add the mascarpone and continue to beat, this time on a medium speed, for about 30 seconds, until combined. Do not overbeat. Refrigerate the icing until just before you are ready to use it. Ice each cupcake with some of this icing and decorate with sugar-dipped grapes (see below) if you like.

Sugar-dipped grapes

12 red grapes
1 egg white
granulated sugar

Dip each grape in the egg white and then roll in granulated sugar. Leave to set for a little while before using to decorate the cupcakes. As this decoration includes raw egg whites, remember not to give them to pregnant women or children.

Salted Caramel Cupcakes

Makes 12 regular cupcakes

110g unsalted butter, at room temperature
225g caster sugar, preferably golden
2 large eggs, free-range or organic
1 teaspoon good-quality vanilla extract
120ml semi-skimmed milk
150g self-raising flour
125g plain flour
1 bar of caramel chocolate, such as Galaxy, broken into 12 pieces

This has become one of our favourite and quite possibly bestselling cupcakes almost overnight. Like Martha, our chef Lisa Chan loves salted caramel, so she was just as keen to make the perfect cupcake version. We have also made this as a giant cupcake, which worked equally well.

Preheat the oven to 180°C/160°C (fan)/350°F/gas 4. Line a 12-hole muffin tray with muffin cases.

Cream the butter and sugar in a bowl until the mixture is pale and smooth. Add the eggs, one at a time, mixing briefly after each addition. This can take a few minutes. Scrape down the sides of the bowl with a rubber spatula to ensure the mixture stays well combined.

Put the vanilla extract and milk into a plastic measuring jug. Combine the two flours in a separate bowl. Add one-third of the flours to the combined butter and sugar mixture and beat well. Pour in one-third of the milk and beat again. Repeat these steps until all the flour and milk has been added.

Carefully and evenly spoon the mixture into the muffin cases. Add one piece of the chocolate to each case and push it in slightly. You will find it sinks to the bottom of the case during baking.

Bake in the centre of the oven for approximately 25 minutes, until slightly raised and golden brown and an inserted skewer comes out clean. Remove from the oven. Leave the cupcakes in the tray for 10 minutes or so, then place carefully on a wire rack to cool. While they are cooling, make the salted caramel buttercream icing (see page 181).

Salted Caramel Buttercream Icing

110g granulated sugar
3 tablespoons water
125ml double cream
1 teaspoon fleur de sel

**200g salted caramel sauce
(see above)**
200g butter, softened
400g icing sugar
**hard caramel sweets, such
as Werther's Original®
or similar, crushed**
fleur de sel

First make the salted caramel sauce. As this is a very hot liquid, you need to be careful when making it.

Place the sugar and water in a clean, medium-sized saucepan. Place it over a medium heat on the hob. Do not stir the mixture at all, as this will cause the sugar syrup to crystallize. Swirl the pan occasionally and gently until all the sugar has dissolved, then turn the heat up to high and let the syrup boil.

While the sugar syrup is boiling, pour the cream into a separate pan and add the fleur de sel. Heat the cream over a medium heat until it starts 'smoking' (at approximately 80°C). Turn the heat down to medium/low and stir occasionally to stop the cream from forming a skin on top. Do not allow it to boil.

Once the sugar syrup turns an amber colour, remove it from the heat and immediately add a small portion of the hot cream to the pan. Stir quickly with a wooden spoon to prevent it sticking to the bottom of the pan. Be careful when adding the cream, as it will bubble up, rise very quickly, let off steam and may splutter.

Add the remaining cream in small amounts, stirring constantly. Once all the cream is incorporated, pour the sauce into a bowl and set it aside to cool.

Once the caramel sauce is cool, beat it with the butter. Add half the icing sugar and beat again, then add the rest of the sugar and beat until smooth.

Ice each cupcake with some of the buttercream and sprinkle some of the crushed sweets and a little fleur de sel over each one.

Natural Red Velvet Cupcakes

Makes 12 regular cupcakes

FOR THE BEETROOT PURÉE
1 raw beetroot (approximately 140g)
35g frozen raspberries
½ tablespoon apple cider vinegar
½ tablespoon cold water

FOR THE CAKE
185g self-raising flour
a pinch of salt
30g dark chocolate (at least 70% cocoa solids)
60g unsalted butter
150g golden caster sugar
2 eggs
1 teaspoon good-quality vanilla extract
60ml buttermilk (or 55ml milk plus the juice of ½ lemon)
1¼ teaspoons natural red food colouring
115g beetroot purée (see above)

Red velvet cupcakes seem to be one of the nation's favourites, but until now we have never made them, as they require so much red food colouring that they go against our principles. An all-natural version has proved elusive … until now! Our chef Lisa Chan, closely assisted by all of us in the bakery as tasters, finally created this fantastic natural version and we are all very excited!

Preheat the oven to 180°C/160°C (fan)/350°F/gas 4. Line a 12-hole muffin tray with muffin cases.

To make the purée, peel the beetroots and dice into cubes. Place in a food processor with the frozen raspberries, apple cider vinegar and water. Process for 5 minutes, scraping down the sides every couple of minutes to make sure everything is incorporated. Place the purée in a bowl and set aside.

Sift the flour and salt into a bowl and set aside.

Break the chocolate into small pieces and melt, either in the microwave on a medium heat at 10–20 second intervals and stirring well in between, or in a heatproof bowl over a pan of simmering water on the hob, making sure the bowl doesn't touch the water. Be careful not to burn the chocolate. Keep warm and set aside.

Place the butter, sugar, eggs and vanilla into a bowl and beat with an electric hand beater on a medium to high speed for 4–5 minutes, until light and fluffy. Pour in the melted chocolate and beat on a low speed until well combined.

Pour in the buttermilk and natural food colouring and beat on a low speed until well mixed. Add the beetroot purée to the mixture and fold in gently.

Divide the mixture evenly between the muffin cases and bake in the oven for 15–18 minutes, or until an inserted skewer comes out clean. Remove from the oven. Allow the cakes to cool in the tray for about 10 minutes, then turn out onto a wire rack to cool completely. Ice with the cream chees icing (see page 184).

Cream Cheese Icing

40g unsalted butter, at room temperature
80g cream cheese
juice of ¼ lemon
280g icing sugar
red sanding sugar, to decorate (optional)

Place the butter, cream cheese, lemon juice and half the icing
sugar in a bowl. Beat with an electric hand beater on a low speed
until all the ingredients are combined. Add the remaining icing
sugar and beat again on a low speed until all is well mixed,
then turn the beater to a high speed and beat the icing well for
3–4 minutes, or until it is white and fluffy.

Ice each cupcake with the icing and either leave undecorated
or sprinkle a little red sanding sugar over them.

Gluten-free Chocolate and Almond Cupcakes

We are constantly asked for gluten-free cupcakes and recently developed these with the help of our manager, Faye. They have become a popular addition to our counters.

Makes 12 regular cupcakes

125g unsalted butter
125g dark chocolate (at least 70% cocoa solids)
4 large eggs, preferably free-range or organic, separated
125g golden caster sugar
125g ground almonds

Preheat the oven to 180°C/160°C (fan)/350°F/gas 4. Line a 12-hole muffin tray with muffin cases.

Melt the butter and chocolate in a heatproof bowl over a pan of simmering water on the hob, stirring continuously and making sure the bowl doesn't touch the water. Allow to cool.

Whisk the egg yolks and sugar until the mixture is light and fluffy, then fold in the ground almonds with a metal spoon.

In a separate bowl, beat the egg whites until they have soft peaks. Fold the egg yolk and sugar mixture into the egg whites, along with the cooled chocolate and butter.

Carefully and evenly divide the mixture between the cases and bake in the oven for about 20 minutes, or until an inserted skewer comes out clean. These cakes do have a fairly dense consistency. Remove from the oven and allow them to cool in the tray for about 10 minutes, then turn out onto a wire rack to cool completely.

Chocolate Buttercream Icing

350g dark chocolate (at least 70% cocoa solids)
225g unsalted butter, at room temperature
250g icing sugar, sifted
1 tablespoon semi-skimmed milk
1 teaspoon good-quality vanilla extract
flaked almonds and gold sugar stars, to decorate

Break the chocolate into small pieces and melt, either in the microwave on a medium heat at 10–20 second intervals and stirring well in between, or in a heatproof bowl over a pan of simmering water on the hob, making sure the bowl doesn't touch the water. Be careful not to burn the chocolate. Leave to cool slightly.

Beat the butter, icing sugar, milk and vanilla with an electric hand beater until smooth. Add the melted chocolate and beat until thick and creamy.

When the cupcakes are completely cool, ice each one with the chocolate buttercream and decorate with flaked almonds and gold sugar stars.

Chocolate bombs

Makes 16 regular or
48 mini cupcakes

FOR THE SPONGE
**115g good-quality dark
chocolate (70% cocoa
solids if possible)**
**85g unsalted butter, at room
temperature**
175g soft brown sugar
2 large eggs, separated
185g plain flour
¾ teaspoon baking powder
**¾ teaspoon bicarbonate of
soda**
a pinch of salt
**250ml semi-skimmed milk,
at room temperature**
**1 teaspoon good-quality
vanilla extract**

These marshmallow-topped chocolate cupcakes are quite time-consuming and fiddly to make, but they are certainly worth the effort. Allow yourself plenty of time, and be warned – they may take a few attempts to get right.

Preheat the oven to 190°C/170°C (fan)/375°F/gas mark 5. Line a mini cupcake or muffin tin with muffin cases.

Break the chocolate into small pieces and melt, either in the microwave on a medium heat at 10–20 second intervals and stirring well in between, or by putting in a bowl over a pan of boiling water on the hob, making sure the pan doesn't touch the water. Be careful not to burn the chocolate. Leave to cool slightly.

Cream the butter and sugar together with an electric hand beater until pale and smooth. In a separate bowl and with clean beaters, beat the egg yolks for several minutes. Slowly add the egg yolks to the creamed butter and sugar and beat well.

Add the melted chocolate and beat well.

Combine the flour, baking powder, bicarbonate of soda and salt. In a jug, combine the milk and vanilla. Add the flour mixture to the chocolate, butter and sugar, alternating with the milk and vanilla and beating very well after each addition.

In a clean bowl, whisk the egg whites until soft peaks start to form. Carefully fold the egg whites into the main batter using a metal spoon. Do not beat or you will take all the air out of the cake.

Spoon the mixture equally into the tins until they are about two-thirds full. The cakes will rise considerably in the oven. The batter will be of a fairly liquid consistency, so take care when spooning out – it can end up being very messy.

Bake in the oven for 20–25 minutes for the regular size or approximately 15 minutes for mini cupcakes, until an inserted skewer comes out clean. Leave in their tins for 10 minutes or so, then place on a wire rack to cool, before topping with Marshmallow Topping and coating with chocolate (see pages 190–1).

Chocolate Coating

380g dark chocolate (at least 70% cocoa solids), broken into small pieces or chips
3 tablespoons vegetable oil

Melt the dark chocolate with the oil, either in the microwave on a medium heat at 10–20 second intervals and stirring well in between, or in a heatproof bowl over a pan of simmering water on the hob, making sure the bowl doesn't touch the water. Be careful not to burn the chocolate. Once it is melted and a smooth liquid, pour into a jug or wide-brimmed glass with a height of at least 15cm. Set aside to cool while you make the marshmallow topping.

350g granulated sugar
60ml water
3 large egg whites
¼ teaspoon cream of tartar
1 teaspoon good-quality vanilla extract

Fill a medium pan with water to a depth of approximately 2cm and place it over a low heat so that it is barely simmering.

Place the sugar, water, egg whites and cream of tartar in a medium to large heatproof bowl. Beat the mixture for 1 minute, using an electric hand beater on high speed, until it is opaque, white and foamy.

Place the bowl over the pan of water. The water should have steam coming from the top, with only a few bubbles appearing. Immediately start beating again on a high speed and continue for a further 12–13 minutes. During this time, check that the water in the pan is at a gentle simmer. If it starts boiling, turn down the heat and add a little cold water to the pan. (If the bowl is heated too much the mixture will start to cook at the bottom and you'll get small particles throughout your marshmallow topping.)

After 12–13 minutes, the mixture should form stiff peaks that stand straight up when the beaters are stopped and removed. Remove the bowl from the pan, add the vanilla and continue beating on high speed for a further 2 minutes. During this time, the mixture will thicken further and become shinier.

Transfer the topping into a large piping bag with a large round piping tip (or cut off the tip so there is approximately a 1cm circle when piped).

Lay the cupcakes out on a flat board and pipe a spiral of filling on to each one, approximately 5cm high so that it creates a cone shape. Place the board with the cupcakes in the freezer to cool for 20–30 minutes.

When you're ready to coat the cakes, ensure the chocolate coating is a smooth liquid with no lumps and is cool to the touch. If the mix is too hot it will melt the marshmallow topping.

Remove the cakes from the freezer. Holding each cupcake by the base, dip the marshmallow top into the chocolate until all the topping is covered, then remove and let any excess chocolate drip off upside down for a few seconds. Turn back upright and set aside for approximately 15 minutes to let the chocolate set.

Cheese Dog Treats

Dogs are always welcome at Primrose Bakery. We seem only to employ staff who also love dogs, and the sight of a puppy or a cute dog in the shop means everyone stops work and rushes upstairs to see it. Martha's dog Charlie, a miniature dachshund, is our shop mascot, so it seemed very natural that in our Christmas chapter we should include some dog treats (although they can, in fact, be eaten by humans as well). Store any uneaten biscuits in an airtight container for up to a week.

Makes 32 medium-sized biscuits

10g unsalted butter
60ml chicken stock
30g rolled oats
55g brown rice flour
5g golden caster sugar
1 beef stock cube, crumbled
25g grated Cheddar
190g plain flour, plus more for dusting
30ml milk
1 egg

Preheat the oven to 160°C/140°C (fan)/300°F/gas 2. Line a baking tray with parchment paper.

Melt the butter, either in the microwave on a medium heat at 10–20 second intervals and stirring well in between, or in a heatproof bowl over a pan of simmering water on the hob, making sure the bowl doesn't touch the water. Remove from the heat, pour the chicken stock into the melted butter, then add the rolled oats, stir and set aside for 10 minutes.

Put the rice flour, sugar, crumbled stock cube, cheese and flour into a separate bowl and make a well in the centre.

Pour in the milk, add the egg, then add the oat mixture to the dry mixture and stir all the ingredients together with a wooden spoon to make a dough.

Turn the dough out onto a lightly floured surface – if it is a little sticky, add a little more flour when rolling. Roll the dough out to 5mm thick and cut out into the desired shapes (we used a dog-bone shaped cutter).

Place the biscuits on the baking tray and bake in the oven for 20–25 minutes, or until they are firm to the touch. Remove from the oven and cool on the tray for 10 minutes, before transferring to wire racks to cool completely.

Pumpkin Dog Treats

Makes approximately 18–20 medium-sized biscuits

320g plain flour, plus a little more for dusting
170g puréed pumpkin (you can buy this in tins in supermarkets)
1 egg
¼ teaspoon salt
1 chicken stock cube, crumbled

Preheat the oven to 160°C/140°C (fan)/300°F/gas 2. Line a baking tray with parchment paper.

Sift the flour into a bowl and make a well in the centre. Put the pumpkin, egg, salt and crumbled stock cube into a seperate bowl and mix well. Pour this mixture into the well in the flour.

Mix with a wooden spoon to make a dough. Turn the dough out onto a lightly floured surface and roll out to 5mm thickness. Cut out the desired shapes (we used a cat-shaped cutter) and place them on the baking tray.

Bake in the oven for 20–25 minutes, or until firm to the touch. Remove from the oven and cool on the tray for 10 minutes before transferring to wire racks to cool completely.

Chocolate Honeycomb

This delicious treat would make an excellent present, wrapped up in a gift bag tied with ribbon (although it might be hard to stop eating it while you are wrapping it). Don't be put off by the need for a candy thermometer – they are very simple to use.

oil spray
60g honey
60g golden syrup
200g golden caster sugar
1 tablespoon water
20g bicarbonate of soda
200g dark chocolate (70% cocoa solids if possible)

Line a baking tray with parchment paper and lightly spray the paper with oil.

Put the honey, golden syrup, sugar and water into a pan and place over a medium heat on the hob. Bring to the boil, swirling the pot occasionally. Using a candy thermometer, boil the syrup until it reaches 145°C.

Remove from the heat and add the bicarbonate of soda, stirring quickly as it will start to foam. Pour the mixture immediately onto the prepared tray and set aside to cool. Once it has cooled completely, break it into bite-sized pieces.

Break the chocolate into small pieces and melt, either in the microwave on a medium heat at 10–20 second intervals and stirring well in between, or in a heatproof bowl over a pan of simmering water on the hob, making sure the bowl doesn't touch the water. Be careful not to burn the chocolate. Remove from the heat.

Dip each piece of honeycomb into the chocolate. Remove, using a fork, letting the excess drip off, and place on a piece of parchment paper to set.

Once the chocolate honeycomb has set, either pack in cellophane bags to use as gifts or store in an airtight container although these are best eaten on the day.

Mint Marshmallows

Makes one 20cm square, to be
cut into the desired number of
pieces

200g cornflour
200g icing sugar
20g powdered gelatine
185ml cold water
240g granulated white sugar
95g golden syrup
30g liquid glucose
2 egg whites
2 teaspoons peppermint
    flavouring
6–10 drops of red food
    colouring

*A classic Christmas treat, these candy-cane coloured marshmallows
would be the perfect gift, or simply something to enjoy while
wrapping presents or watching a Christmas film on TV.*

Lightly grease a 20cm square baking tin and line with parchment
paper.

Sift the cornflour and icing sugar into a bowl. This will be the
marshmallow coating, to help minimize its stickiness. Re-sift a
generous amount of this mixture into the prepared tin, to
approximately 3–4mm in depth. Set aside.

In a bowl, mix the powdered gelatine with 125ml of cold water,
stir and set aside to hydrate for 10 minutes.

Put the sugar, golden syrup, liquid glucose and 60ml of water
into a pan. Place over a high heat on the hob, swirling the pan
occasionally to ensure that the ingredients are dissolved and
combined. Bring to the boil and place a candy thermometer in
the liquid. Once the sugar mixture is boiling, do not stir with any
utensils as this will cause the sugar syrup to recrystallize. Dip a
pastry brush in a cup of cold water and brush down the sides of
the pan every few minutes. Once the syrup reaches 'soft ball'
stage, at 115°C, remove the pan from the heat and stir in the
gelatine until it has all dissolved.

While the sugar syrup is heating, place the egg whites in the
mixer bowl of, ideally, a stand mixer with a whisk attachment
(otherwise use an electric hand beater). Once the sugar syrup
reaches 112°C whisk the egg whites at high speed until they form
firm, but not dry, peaks. Reduce the speed to low/medium and
pour the sugar/gelatine mixture slowly in a thin stream into the
egg whites then continue whisking on a medium speed for a
further 10 minutes, or until the mixing bowl is cool to touch.
During this time add the peppermint flavouring to the mixture.

Once the mixture has cooled, pour into the prepared tin,
spreading it out evenly. Working quickly, place drops of red food
colouring over the top of the marshmallow. Using a toothpick,
skewer or flat-bladed knife, swirl the food colouring into the
marshmallow mixture to create a marble effect.

Let the marshmallow sit uncovered for at least 3 hours, or
until set. Cover and let it continue to set overnight. Cut the
marshmallows into the desired size using a pair of scissors and
roll in the remaining marshmallow coating.

Store any uneaten marshmallows in an airtight container. They
should keep well for a few days.

Guinness Cake

Makes one 23cm cake

FOR THE CAKE

175g unsalted butter, at room temperature
315g dark soft brown sugar
75g cocoa powder
300ml Guinness (or stout)
260g plain flour
¼ teaspoon baking powder
1½ teaspoons bicarbonate of soda
3 large eggs, preferably free-range or organic

FOR THE ICING

300ml double cream
3 tablespoons Guinness (or stout)
2 tablespoons icing sugar

Our chef Julia originally developed this cake for St Patrick's Day, but we thought it would make a good cake either to give as a Christmas gift or to serve at a pre-Christmas celebration. In both flavour and presentation it should resemble a pint of Guinness!

Preheat the oven to 160°C/140°C (fan)/300°F/gas 2. Grease and line one 23cm-deep cake tin.

Cream the butter and sugar together in a large bowl. Put the cocoa powder into a separate bowl and gradually stir in the Guinness. In a third bowl, combine the flour, baking powder and bicarbonate of soda.

Add the eggs to the creamed butter and sugar and beat well. Add half the flour mixture to the bowl and beat well, then add half the cocoa/Guinness mix and beat again. Repeat the process so that all the cake ingredients are combined.

Pour the mixture into the prepared tin and bake in the centre of the oven for about 1 hour, or until the cake is pulling away from the sides of the tin. It is very important that the cake is not overcooked – it should be very moist.

Remove from the oven and allow to cool in the tin for about 10 minutes, then turn out onto a wire rack to cool fully.

Make the icing by putting the cream into a bowl with the Guinness and icing sugar and whisking to soft peaks. Ice the top of the cake, to create the 'cream' effect of a pint of Guinness, and serve. Any uneaten cake will need to be stored in the fridge because of the fresh cream in the icing.

ACKNOWLEDGEMENTS

Once again, and in fact more than ever for this book, we are indebted to all our staff at Primrose Bakery, who have contributed recipes, ideas and time to this book and to running the bakery while we have been busy writing. In particular we must thank Faye MacGregor, Sally Humphreys, Julia Murphy-Buske, Lisa Chan, Laura Rogers and Rachel Wicking. We also have two Mongolian chefs, Baggi and Manda, who have been with us a very long time and their hard and efficient work day after day often goes unrecognized.

Our lovely agent Charlotte Robertson has again worked very hard on our behalf and often operates as the go-between for us and our publishers! At Square Peg, our editor Caroline McArthur has been a pleasure to work with and has made the whole process very easy. Our photographer, Yuki Sugiura, has helped a third time to bring the book to life with her amazing photographs. Friederike Huber, Alice Whiting, Mariko Ueno, Rosemary Davidson, Fiona Murphy, Kim Lightbody and Lisa Chan have also been key to the production of this book.

Our family and friends always contribute greatly to our books and to the bakery itself, with their ideas, suggestions and contributions – Kevin, Thomas and Ned Thomas, Daisy and Millie Heath, Roger and Marlene Glover, Martin and Kerrin Glover, Caroline Moorehead, Jeremy and Camilla Swift, Daniel Swift, Leo Swift Roiphe, Ray, Rachel and Sam Winters and Andrew Newland.

Special thanks this time must go to Kinder Aggugini, Gabriel Toumazis, Ashleigh Thompson and Kate Miller for the teenage party chapter, Frances, Rodolphe, Rex and Maud Von Hofmannsthal for the boy's birthday party chapter, Zaim, Chichi and Candice Kamal for the girl's party chapter, Georgia Goldstein for the girl's party chapter and everyone at Sipsmith, Lucky Seven, Crazy Homies and Rococo.

INDEX

Aviation cupcakes 143–4

Baklava 110
Beetroot purée 182
Bellini cupcakes 137
Black sesame crisps with tuna 130
bourbon whiskey
   Old fashioned cupcakes 164
Bubblegum buttercream icing 18
Bubblegum cupcakes 17
buttercream icing *see* icing

cakes
   Chocolate and marshmallow layer
     cake 170–73
   Chocolate chilli moustache cake 62
   Coconut and elderflower cake 73
   Confetti cake 25 6
   Green tea marble loaf cake with
     white chocolate icing 127
   Guinness cake 201
   Jasmine cake 114 15
   Lemon and rose layer cake 93
   Orange, pistachio and almond cake 94
   Plum wine drizzle loaf 129
   Puffed rice doughnut cake 14
   Puffed rice gumball cake 36
   Tres leches cake 55
   see also cupcakes
Candied oranges 163
Caramel sauce 94
Champagne buttercream icing 137
cheese
   Cheese dog treats 192
   Cheese quesadillas 66
   Cream cheese icing 184
   Mexican corn on the cob 69
Cherry buttercream icing 116

chocolate
   Chocolate and marshmallow
     layer cake 170–73
   Chocolate bombs 188–91
   Chocolate buttercream icing
     62, 172, 187
   Chocolate chilli and coffee ice
     cream sandwiches 61
   Chocolate chilli moustache cake 62
   Chocolate flapjacks 80
   Chocolate honeycomb 196
   Gluten-free chocolate and almond
     cupcakes 187
   Mexican chocolate spiced cupcakes
     58–9
   Milk chocolate icing 39
   Rocky Road cupcakes 79
   Rose and violet mini chocolate bombs
     99–100
   Sake ganache filling 120
   Spiced chocolate buttercream icing 59
   White chocolate buttercream icing 127
   White chocolate cupcakes 20–23
   White chocolate icing 23
Christmas trifle cupcakes 175
Club sandwiches 88
'cocktails'
   Roy Rogers cocktail 48
   Shirley Temple cocktail 48
coconut
   Coconut and elderflower cake 73
   Lime and coconut macaroons 83
   Orange and coconut slice 82
Cola cupcakes 40
Cola icing 40
Confetti cake 25–6
Courgette and ginger loaf 85
Cream cheese icing 184
Cucumber mint cupcakes 159

cupcakes
   Aviation cupcakes 143–4
   Bellini cupcakes 137
   Bubblegum cupcakes 17–18
   Chocolate bombs 188 91
   Christmas trifle cupcakes 175
   Cola cupcakes 40
   Cucumber mint cupcakes 159
   Eton mess cupcakes 74–7
   Gin and tonic cupcakes 138
   Gluten-free chocolate and almond
     cupcakes 187
   Grape cupcakes 42
   Margarita cupcakes 155
   Mexican chocolate spiced cupcakes 58
   Mini cherry blossom cupcakes 116
   Mojito cupcakes 152
   Moscow mule cupcakes 147–8
   Mulled wine cupcakes 176
   Natural red velvet cupcakes 182–4
   Negroni cupcakes 160–63
   Old fashioned cupcakes 164
   Peanut butter and jelly cupcakes 38
   Pear Martini cupcakes 151
   Rocky Road cupcakes 79
   Rose and violet mini chocolate bombs
     99
   Salted caramel cupcakes 178–81
   Strawberry Daiquiri cupcakes 154
   Summercup cupcakes 159
   Tequila sunrise cupcakes 156
   White Cargo cupcakes 141
   White chocolate cupcakes 20–23
Custard buttercream icing 175

Date bars 96
dog treats
   Cheese dog treats 192
   Pumpkin dog treats 195

Elderflower buttercream icing 73
Eton mess cupcakes 74–7

Fairy bread 31
Flapjacks, Chocolate 80

gin
    Aviation cupcakes 143–4
    Gin and tonic cupcakes 138
    Gin and tonic icing 138
    Gin and vanilla buttercream icing 141
    White Cargo cupcakes 141
Gluten free chocolate and almond
        cupcakes 187
grapes
    Grape cupcakes 42
    Grape icing 42
    Sugar-dipped grapes 176
Green tea marble loaf cake with white
        chocolate icing 127
Green tea scones with lemon cream 126
Guacamole 67
Guinness cake 201

Hot dogs 49

ice-cream
    Chocolate chilli and coffee ice-cream
        sandwiches 61
    Ice-cream floats 30
    Sprinkle covered ice-cream
        sandwiches 29
icing
    Bubblegum buttercream icing 18
    Champagne buttercream icing 137
    Cherry buttercream icing 116
    Chocolate buttercream icing 62, 172,
        187
    Cola icing 40
    Cream cheese icing 184

Custard buttercream icing 175
    Elderflower buttercream icing 73
    Gin and tonic icing 138
    Gin and vanilla buttercream icing 141
    Grape icing 42
Jasmine and vanilla buttercream icing
        115, 127
    Lime and rum buttercream icing 152
    Lime and tequila buttercream icing
        155
    Lime and vodka buttercream icing 148
    Marshmallow icing 173
    Milk chocolate icing 39
    Negroni buttercream icing 163
    Old fashioned icing 164
    Orange and tequila buttercream icing
        156
    Orange icing 82
    Pink vanilla buttercream icing 26
    Rose petal icing 93
    Rum icing 154
    Salted caramel buttercream icing 181
    Spiced chocolate buttercream icing 59
    Spiced mascarpone icing 176
    Summercup buttercream icing 159
    Violet liqueur buttercream icing 144
    White chocolate buttercream icing 127
    White chocolate icing 23
    see also toppings

Jasmine and vanilla buttercream icing
        115, 127
Jasmine cake 114–15

Lemon and rose layer cake 93
Lemon cream 126
lemonade
    Mint lemonade 109
    Pink lemonade 109
    Pomegranate lemonade 109

limes
    Lime and coconut macaroons 83
    Lime and rum buttercream icing 152
    Lime and tequila buttercream icing
        155
    Lime and vodka buttercream icing 148
    Mojito cupcakes 152
    Strawberry Daiquiri cupcakes 154

macaroons
    Lime and coconut macaroons 83
    Plum wine macaroons 122
    Sake macaroons 120
Margarita cupcakes 155
marshmallow
    Chocolate bombs 188 91
    Marshmallow icing 173
    Marshmallow topping 100
    Mint marshmallows 198
    Rose and violet mini chocolate bombs
        99–100
    Chocolate and marshmallow layer
        cake 170–73
mascarpone
    Mascarpone filling 74
    Spiced mascarpone icing 176
Meringue 77
    Rose and pistachio mini meringues
        103
Mexican chocolate spiced cupcakes
        58–9
Mexican corn on the cob 69
Milk chocolate icing 39
Mini cherry blossom cupcakes 116
Mint lemonade 109
Mint marshmallows 198
Mint tea 110
Mojito cupcakes 152
Moscow mule cupcakes 147–8
muffins

Summer savoury muffins 86
Mulled wine cupcakes 176

Natural red velvet cupcakes 182–4
Ned's orange and cinnamon fruit salad
    104
Negroni buttercream icing 163
Negroni cupcakes 160–63

Old fashioned cupcakes 164
oranges
    Candied oranges 163
    Ned's orange and cinnamon fruit salad
        104
    Orange and coconut slice 82
    Orange and tequila buttercream icing
        156
    Orange, pistachio and almond cake
        94

Peanut butter and jelly cupcakes
    38–9
Pear Martini cupcakes 151
Pink lemonade 109
Pink vanilla buttercream icing 26
Pitta bread and hummus 110
Plum wine 132
Plum wine drizzle loaf 129
Plum wine filling 122
Plum wine macaroons 122
Pomegranate ice cubes 108
Pomegranate lemonade 109
popcorn
    Salted caramel popcorn 46
Puffed rice doughnut cake 14
Puffed rice gumball cake 36
Pumpkin dog treats 195

raspberries
    Eton mess cupcakes 74–7

Raspberry cream topping 77
Rocky Road cupcakes 79
Rose and pistachio mini meringues 103
Rose and violet mini chocolate bombs
    99–100
Rose petal icing 93
Roy Rogers cocktail 48
rum
    Lime and rum buttercream icing 152
    Mojito cupcakes 152
    Rum icing 154
    Strawberry Daiquiri cupcakes 154

Sake ganache filling 120
Sake macaroons 120
Salted caramel buttercream icing 181
Salted caramel cupcakes 178 81
Salted caramel popcorn 46
sandwiches
    Chocolate chilli and coffee ice cream
        sandwiches 61
    Club sandwiches 88
    Sprinkle covered ice cream
        sandwiches 29
scones
    Green tea scones with lemon cream
        126
Shirley Temple cocktail 48
Spiced chocolate buttercream icing 59
Spiced mascarpone icing 176
Sprinkle covered ice cream sandwiches
    29
Strawberry Daiquiri cupcakes 154
Summer savoury muffins 86
Summercup buttercream icing 159
Summercup cupcakes 159

tequila
    Lime and tequila buttercream icing
        155

Margarita cupcakes 155
Orange and tequila buttercream icing
    156
Tequila sunrise cupcakes 156
toppings
    Marshmallow topping 100
    Raspberry cream topping 77
    see also icing
Tres leches cake 55
Turkish delight 110

Violet liqueur buttercream icing 144
vodka
    Lime and vodka buttercream icing 148
    Moscow mule cupcakes 147 8
    Pear Martini cupcakes 151

White Cargo cupcakes 141
White chocolate buttercream icing 127
White chocolate cupcakes 20 23
White chocolate icing 23

SWEET!
SWEET!
LISA
THOMAS
MARTHA
SWIFT
PRIMROSE BAKERY
CELEBRATIONS
OPEN

Published by Square Peg 2013

10 9 8 7 6 5 4 3 2 1

The Random House Group Limited Reg. No. 954009

Addresses for companies within The Random House Group Limited can be found at: www.randomhouse.co.uk

A CIP catalogue record for this book is available from the British Library

ISBN 978 0 22 408691 2

Photography: Yuki Sugiura
Design: Friederike Huber
Styling: Alice Whiting, Lisa Thomas and Martha Swift
Copy editing: Annie Lee
Proofreading: Natasha Martyn-Johns

Printed and bound in China by C&C Offset Printing Co., Ltd

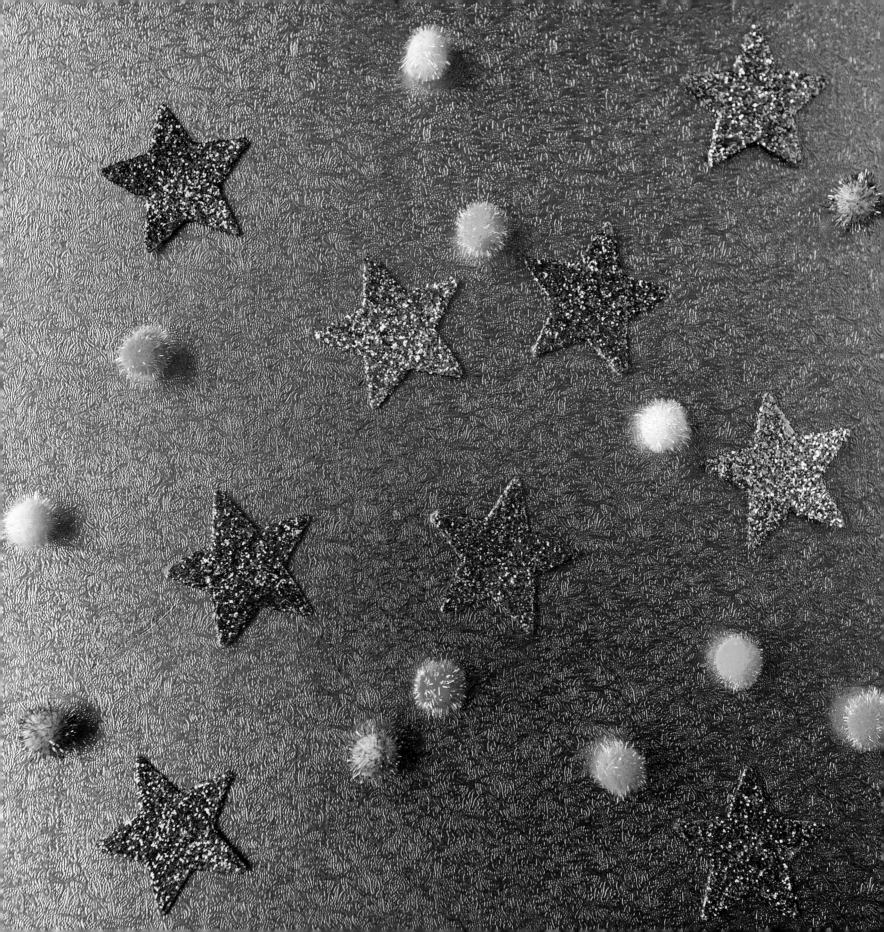